D1263214

JAKE LAMAR
BOURGEOIS BLUES

An American Memoir

SUMMIT BOOKS

New York London Toronto Sydney Tokyo Singapore

SUMMIT BOOKS
Simon & Schuster Building
Rockefeller Center
1230 Avenue of the Americas
New York, New York 10020

Copyright © 1991 by Jake Lamar

SUMMIT BOOKS and colophon are trademarks
of Simon & Schuster Inc.

Designed by Laurie Jewell
Manufactured in the United States of America

10 9 8 7 6 5 4 3 2 1

Library of Congress Cataloging in Publication data
Lamar, Jake.
     Bourgeois blues : an American memoir / Jake Lamar.
        p.   cm.
     1.Lamar, Jake.   2.Journalists—United States—Biography.
     3.Afro-American journalists—Biography.   I.Title.
     PN4874.L2A3   1991
     070'.92—dc20   91-23240
     [B]   CIP

ISBN: 0-671-69191-0

AUTHOR'S NOTE

THIS BOOK is neither fiction nor journalism, but a work of the memory; and while subject to memory's vagaries, it is faithful to the stories I remember. One minor character is a composite of several men I've known, and the names of most people outside my family have been changed.

I am especially grateful to Tamara Heimarck, Darcy Frey and Hugh Browne for their immeasurable generosity. I'd also like to thank Kristine Dahl, a champion of this book from the start; Dominick Anfuso, for his graceful and perceptive editing; all the good friends who offered support and guidance; and Joan Whitehead, for sowing the seeds.

For my family

"Play the game, but don't believe in it—that much you owe yourself. Even if it lands you in a strait jacket or a padded cell. Play the game, but play it your own way—part of the time at least. Play the game, but raise the ante, my boy."

—RALPH ELLISON
Invisible Man

Love comes in very strange packages.

—JAMES BALDWIN

PART 1

FOR A LONG TIME I pretended my father was dead. I blocked him out of my mind, rarely mentioning him to friends or discussing him with family. I craved a life in neutral, a simple, orderly life; a life insulated from the turbulence I associated with my father. No ugly confrontations, no financial catastrophes. I just wanted to do my job, hang out with my friends, pay my bills on time. I submerged myself in everydayness. Everydayness, I thought, would be my deliverance. Pretending Dad did not exist made it easier for me to get through the day; and far easier for me to believe that I was nothing like him. But, at twenty-seven, I was finally coming to grips with the fact that my father and I were, naturally, inevitably, the same thing, that most inconvenient of Americans: a black man who didn't know his place.

It was the fall of 1988, a drizzly night in mid-November, and my insomnia was worse than ever. I poured myself a glass of Wild Turkey, popped a Thelonious Monk compact disc into the CD player, and stretched out on the couch. I was comfortable in my cocoon, a one-bedroom five-flight walk-up on 74th Street, just off Columbus Avenue, the heart of Manhattan's Quiche Belt—a neighborhood of sleek, overpriced restaurants, trendy boutiques and desperate panhandlers—where a tiny apartment such as mine, costing $875 a month, was considered a steal. I closed my eyes and zoned out to the music. As the bourbon warmed my insides, Monk was playing "Crepuscule with Nellie," conjuring sounds jagged and rapturous. These were the times when I felt abstracted from myself, when the past became present and I imagined I could hear my father's voice inside my head; when I wondered how his mind had shaped my mind, where my father's way of thinking ended and my own way began.

I remembered my father as a man of furious contradictions. He had an irresistible charm that made him the center of attention at any gathering; yet he was given to long periods of impenetrable gloom. He was a man who loved to drink and party; and a workaholic who often stayed up all night at the dining room table laboring over his latest business projects. When he played with his children, he displayed the enthusiasm of a kid himself. But in an instant he could explode into terrifying, violent rages. He was a man of towering arrogance who nonetheless was tormented by a sense of inferiority that bordered on self-loathing. Race and class were at the core of one of the most painful conflicts in Dad's life, the struggle to reconcile the world in which he had been born—poor, Southern, black—with the world in which he tried to establish himself, one that was wealthy, privileged, white.

For me, the lines between the black and white worlds had always been more blurred. Growing up, I took my race for granted. I was born in 1961, during the heyday of the civil rights movement. At school, I was taught African American history and read African American literature. At home, I was bred to believe that I was at least the equal of any other person, black or white. I enjoyed advantages that most blacks of my father's generation—and many of my

own—could only have dreamed of: a middle-class upbring-
ing, a private-school education, a Harvard degree, a job
writing on national affairs at *Time* magazine. I tried to live
my life by Dr. King's credo, judging people not by the color
of their skin but by the content of their character. And I
simply assumed that all reasonable human beings did the
same.

But the older I got, the more I found that the color of
my skin was the dominant factor in how people judged
me—and judgments were getting harsher all the time.
Black and white people alike had certain notions about
every aspect of my life: how I should dress and talk; how I
was supposed to choose my friends and lovers; where I
should live; how and what I should write. There were black
people who saw American life as a perpetual race war and
expected me to choose sides. There were white people who
presumed that what I wanted was to be just like them, and
who were dismayed to learn otherwise. "You know what
your problem is, Jake?" a black friend once said. "You're
too white for black people and too black for white people."
I began to wonder, Was I some sort of freak?

Three in the morning and I still couldn't sleep. I switched
from Monk to a Jimi Hendrix CD. "If the sun refuse to
shine," Hendrix sang, "I don't mind, I don't mind . . ."

I imagined, in my indulgently maudlin state, that Hendrix knew what it was like to live in the gray area, shunned
by black people who couldn't get into his psychedelic vision; patronized by whites like the *Rolling Stone* critic who,
after hearing Hendrix outrock the Claptons and the Town-
shends of the world, wrote, "I'd rather hear Jimi play the
blues."

"Got my own world to look through," Hendrix wailed, "and I ain't gonna copy you!"

Feeling ornery and hollow, I poured myself another glass of Turkey and listened to Hendrix CDs till I was drunk enough to go to bed.

"I'm a private investigator and I'm looking for your father."

The voice on the phone managed to be at once friendly and brusque, affecting the practiced informality of a telephone solicitor. Not at all how I'd imagined a private eye would sound. It was bad enough that the ringing phone had jolted me awake at ten of eight in the morning. This unctuous voice only rattled me more. As the detective babbled about shady business deals my father had allegedly been involved in some ten years earlier, all I wanted was to get him off the phone as fast as possible. "I've been trying to track down your dad for quite some time now," the detective said jauntily. "Do you know how I could get in touch with him?"

In a glacial monotone intended to preclude any further discussion, I told the gumshoe the truth: "I haven't seen or heard from my father in five years."

"Five years. Oh my. Well, uh, do you know where he's living? If he's in the city?"

"No."

"Would any other family members know how I could reach him?"

"No."

"Would you happen to know his Social Security number or his birth date?"

"I never knew his Social Security number and I don't remember his birthday."

"Well, uh, just a couple more questions."

"Look, I've got nothing to say to you."

"If you could just—"

"Goodbye."

My hand trembled after I slammed down the receiver. I was furious at this stranger who would ask me to sell out my father. But I was even angrier at my father; angry that after all these years I still couldn't escape him. I hadn't been completely honest with the detective. I knew the town where my father lived in self-imposed exile. I knew that others in the family had been in touch with him. My brother, Bert, had even given me a phone number where my father could be reached. For months, I'd wrestled with the idea of contacting Dad, unable to shake the notion that to make some sense of my own life I would have to try to make some sense of my father's as well. Now a private investigator was looking for Dad. Somebody was out to get him. I would have to talk to my father.

CHAPTER 2

'M AN ESCAPEE from the garbage can," my father said proudly. "That's all I am. They tried to slam the lid down on me. 'Stay in there, boy! Stay down there with the rest of the trash!' But I jumped out at the last second. That's right, man. Just a poor little ole country nigger from Shingley, Georgia, come up here to the big city. I'm not *supposed* to be here. Do you realize that? I'm from Shingley, Georgia—population fifteen, including the cows and the chickens. But I knew when I was a boy I wasn't stayin' in no Shingley, Georgia. Uh-uh. No way. 'Cause I was *smart*. Shit, I was reading at three. You believe that? It's true. Now I look around me, sittin' up here in a six-room apartment in New York City, and sometimes it's like I can hardly believe it. I mean, I'm not *supposed* to be here."

My father reached down and raised the glass of scotch that had been sitting on the floor between his feet. "Of course, I'm ninety-six years old," Dad said as he leaned back on Bert's bed, stretching out his forty-four-year-old legs and smiling his big brash smile, savoring the pungent incongruity of being a man still in the prime of life but endowed with the wisdom of a grizzled nonagenarian, a man who had seen it all at least once and could now kick back and pass on the fruits of his knowledge to his firstborn son and namesake. With a languorous flourish, my father

raised his glass above his head as if to toast me—or himself—and took a long, majestic sip. Sitting cross-legged on
my bed across the room, surrounded by textbooks, notepads and binders, I got set for an extended boozy mono-
logue, another retelling of the Myth of Dad. I listened in a
sort of trancelike state brought on by a mixture of boredom
and awe, pride and pity, curiosity and appreciation—appreciation of a good performance as well as a tingling sense of
gratitude that Dad had chosen me as his audience. These
self-glorifying soliloquies were, after all, nothing if not
lively theater, tours de force fueled by liquor, punctuated
by emphatic gesticulation and boisterous laughs, propelled
by a voice that was an astonishing instrument, now booming with Old Testament fury, now thin and mewling as it
mimicked a lesser set of pipes, now steady and sonorous as
it articulated a deluge of theories, convictions and preju-
dices in tones of unimpeachable reasonableness; it was a
voice that enveloped, a voice that consumed.

This was the day when everything changed, a breezy
Sunday afternoon in early April 1977. Mom was out with
friends; my sister, Felicia, was closeted in her bedroom;
Bert watched TV in the living room. I had been in my
bedroom all afternoon doing homework. I'd heard Dad
walk in the door a half hour earlier, at about four o'clock—
the first time he'd been home since Thursday morning.
Now he sat on Bert's bed wearing a white undershirt, neatly
pressed blue pinstriped pants and his heavy black wing-
tipped Daddy shoes. He was unusually fidgety that day. He
ran a hand through his close-cropped hair, adjusted and
readjusted his black thick-framed eyeglasses, stroked his
trim little mustache with thumb and forefinger. Dad's hands
were long and elegant, his skin dark, leathery. Though a
middle-aged paunch hung over his belt, he was still a pow-

erfully built man. At sixteen, an age when I was just becoming aware of the power of my own body, I couldn't help
wondering if I could take him in a fight.

There was a time, just a few years earlier, when the
click of my father's key in the door was like an alarm to me.
The sound typically occurred in the dead of night. I would
lie in bed awake, waiting for it. If I did manage to drift off
to sleep, it was usually a fitful rest since my ears remained
on constant alert. The sound of the tumbler turning in the
heavy yellow lock instantly jarred me into full consciousness. Then I would wait, staring into the darkness, praying
Dad wouldn't start another fight. If, after half an hour or so,
no outburst occurred, I could finally surrender myself to a
deep sleep. But on those nights when Dad did not come
home at all, I'd spend the entire night suspended between
sleep and wakefulness, waiting for the alarm to sound.

Occasionally, Dad would get home before my bedtime.
This did not diminish my fear. If I was sitting in the living
room when I heard the key in the lock, I'd quickly gather
my belongings and race down the hall to my bedroom. It
was as if I needed time to prepare myself for the sight of
Dad. Eventually, he would knock on my door, step in and
say hi. We would shake hands—our customary way of greeting each other—and exchange a few words before he went
off to the dining room to eat dinner. These early arrivals
home ordinarily portended a quiet night and I slept more
easily.

Some late nights I'd be lying in bed watching television
when the key clicked. I'd jump up, turn off the set, shut out
the light, scurry under the covers and feign sleep. One
night I heard Dad enter my room just as I pulled the sheets
over my shoulders. I opened my eyes ever so slightly and
spied him through my lashes. Dad placed his palm flat on

top of the TV to check its warmth. He looked at me. I shut my eyes tight. He had to know I was faking. I held my breath, waiting for him to say something. All I heard was the sound of the bedroom door closing softly behind him. I whispered a thanks to God.

But in the year and a half since I'd begun high school, Dad had started to get chummy with me, and I had grown less fearful of him. He would wander into my bedroom while I was reading or watching TV, plop down on Bert's bed and talk for hours. I knew that Mom and Felicia and Bert wondered what it was he told me. They teased me for listening to his tales. Yet, I suspected that they envied the intimacy, the exclusivity, of my audiences with Dad.

My father was talking now of his days as an academic phenomenon, of the time in the fifth grade when the teacher was stumped by a math problem and Dad walked up to the blackboard and solved it for her, patiently explaining the solution to the awestruck classroom. The feat was all the more remarkable given that Dad had already been skipped two grades.

"Mathematics," my father said grandly. "Man, I ate that shit up. Ever tell you how I got into college?"

"Yeah," I said, "you've told me."

Without a moment's pause, Dad launched into the story. "Fifteen years old and I was already a senior in high school, head of the damn class. Principal tells me he wants to see me in his office first thing Monday morning—and to bring my mother! So Monday morning Ma and I show up and the principal's looking all nervous and frightened when he answers the door. Sittin' there in his office is this fat, sweaty-faced cracker, says he's some kind of state education officer. And the cracker says to me, 'Boy—according to these here test scores, you the smartest nigra in the state.'

And I say, 'Yessir, that's right.' And that cracker just stared at me for a long time and then he says, 'Boy—the state has decided that we want to send a nigra to college. And that nigra is you.' Man, I almost shit my damn pants. College! The white folks want to send me to college? And I look over at Ma and she's sittin' there lookin' like she's about to bust out crying. And then that flabby-assed cracker says, 'Boy— you can go to any college in the state. *Any college in the state.* Except . . . for the University of Georgia, Georgia Tech, Georgia A & M, Emory . . .' And then Ma says, 'I want my son to go to Morehouse.' Which was just as well since the white folks weren't about to send me anyplace else."

Atlanta's Morehouse was regarded by many as the finest black college in America (some would rank Washington's Howard University higher, but none dared suggest this to my father). Dad excelled there, performing well in his courses, emerging as a popular student leader and earning a reputation as a ladies' man with his conquests at Morehouse's sister school, Spelman College. He also made his first acquaintance with the black bourgeoisie, the wellspoken, carefully tailored sons of ministers, lawyers, doctors and successful businessmen (including, two years ahead of my father, the son of Atlanta's most prominent clergyman, an unpretentious student named Martin Luther King, Jr.). Dad was determined to prove to his more privileged classmates that he was no "ignorant country nigger."

My grandmother was thrilled when Dad told her he was graduating first in his major, business administration. But at the commencement ceremony, the dean mistakenly announced that Jacob V. Lamar had finished second in his field of concentration. "Ma whipped around, grabbed my arm and said, 'Second!'" Dad laughed. "Man, I thought she was gonna start beating me over the head with her handbag." Dad tried to explain that the dean had slipped, but his mother wasn't satisfied until she saw the certificate confirming her son's first-place status.

My grandmother was christened Marjorie Cook in 1913, but everyone called her "Good." Even as a six-year-old, strong-willed and scrupulously well-behaved, growing up in rural Sylvester, Georgia, Good followed her own moral compass. Walking past a neighbor's home one afternoon, Good asked her mother, Miss Liza, about the strange sounds coming out of the house, the muted cries and crashes.

"That's just Mr. Buford beatin' on his wife," Miss Liza said matter-of-factly.

"My husband ain't gonna beat on me!" Good said.

"Why not?"

" 'Cause if he do, I'll leave him."

Good's extraordinary beauty set her apart from the other girls in town. With skin like rich mahogany, high cheekbones and the long, satiny black hair she inherited from her maternal grandfather—a full-blooded Cherokee whose mane was so long, Good remembered, he used to sit on it—she became the most sought-after young woman in Sylvester. But Good was aloof, writing off the boys in town as "common." There was, however, one exception.

My grandfather, the first Jacob Lamar, didn't have much money; but he was a hard worker, supplementing the wages he earned fixing up cars in a downtown garage with any other jobs he could find. And Jacob had style. He drove a nice car and always dressed sharp. To Good, he was that rarity in Sylvester: a real gentleman. Jacob wasn't loud or crude like the others, she thought. He didn't try to lure her into the woods and weaken her defenses with corn liquor, as other boys had fruitlessly attempted. Jacob knew how to court a lady. Every afternoon, he'd show up at Good's high school to drive her home; and every afternoon, he'd bring her one of the big, blood-red apples he knew she loved. She was barely eighteen when they married; he was only a few years older. The newlyweds moved from Sylvester to a small house in nearby Shingley. Within a year, Good was pregnant. The baby kicked so hard and so relentlessly that Good's friends teased her, "You've got a billy goat in there." And so my father—who would be called Jacob like his father, and would also receive a middle name, Virgil— acquired his lifelong nickname, Billy, before he was even born.

Jacob's nasty side began to show. He started staying out late drinking and gambling, staggering home at dawn. The more Jacob exercised his freedom to do what he wanted when he wanted, the more possessive he became of his wife. Poisonously jealous, he saw nearly every man as a threat. One night he flew into a rage because Good, he said, had been overly friendly in greeting another man in town. He accused her of carrying on an affair. She denied it. He hit her, hard.

Jacob said he was sorry for what he had done. He begged his wife to forgive him, promising never to strike her again. Good agreed to give him another chance—exactly one more chance. Miss Liza thought her daughter was being unreasonable. "You just have to put up with it," she said, "and pray your husband don't leave you."

"Why?" Good fumed. "He ain't prayin' I don't leave *him*!"

Jacob soon broke his vow, conjuring up another imaginary infidelity, screaming accusations despite his wife's denials, losing control and slugging her again. That did it. Good packed her bags, picked up her baby and moved back into her parents' home. "My body is all I got," Good told her mother. "And I'm gonna protect it."

It was the summer of 1932, the bleakest period of the Great Depression. Most of the young women my grandmother knew were building large families; her older sister would give birth to nine children. But Good was happy with only one child, one precious offspring who wouldn't have to compete with siblings for his mother's meager resources. Unable to find decent work in Sylvester, Good eventually left Billy with her parents and moved to Augusta. She worked as a shop clerk, a cleaning woman, a baby-sitter, sending the better part of her earnings back home to buy food and clothes for her son.

Miss Liza, meanwhile, lavished attention on her grand-boy. Little Billy could do no wrong in her eyes. Visiting Sylvester, Good noticed that when her son got into mischief, Miss Liza instantly forgave him, never inflicting a punishment or seeking an acknowledgment from Billy that he had done anything bad. Years later, when Good had moved to New York and Billy was on vacation from Morehouse, Miss Liza came North for a week-long visit. Though there was an empty bed for him, seventeen-year-old Billy slept beside his grandmother on the fold-out couch every night. I don't think my father ever loved anyone the way he loved his grandmother. I was eight or nine years old the evening Dad came home from work and Mom told him Miss Liza had died. Dad opened his mouth as if to scream, but no sound emerged; tears suddenly poured from his eyes. Without saying a word, he rushed down the hall to his bedroom and shut the door. It was the first of two times that I would see my father cry.

Soon after his divorce from Good, Jacob remarried. Billy rarely saw his father. Occasionally he would go down to the garage and talk to Jacob while he worked on the cars. When Billy was thirteen, Jacob and his wife moved to another state. My father would never see his father again.

My grandmother often marveled at my resemblance to her first husband. She would stare at me and shake her head: "You're the spittin' image." I had to take her word for it. Not a single snapshot of my grandfather appeared in any of the family photo albums I'd seen. Aside from my grandmother, who rarely went into much detail, no one ever told me anything about Jacob. My father had never, not once, mentioned his father to me.

"I was the angriest man in America!" my father boomed. An hour had passed since he'd first come into the bedroom and started talking that Sunday afternoon. He was telling me, once again, about the summer after he graduated from Morehouse when, just as he had begun working for an Atlanta bank, he received his letter of induction. Despite all the lectures I'd heard Dad deliver on the evils of Communism, the Korean War was, for my father, an unwelcome distraction from the most important matter at hand: his career.

During basic training, Dad became friends with a Creole hell-raiser from Beaumont, Texas, named Philip Doucette. While Dad fancied himself a badass, Phil Doucette was the genuine article. One night the two were at a bar a long way from the base when Phil got into a shouting match with another customer. The hulking, drunken antagonist began screaming that he was going to, quite literally, murder Phil. As Dad tells it, Philip promptly whipped out a straight razor and a pistol. Brandishing a weapon in each hand, he yelled, "Cut or shoot, motherfucker! Cut or shoot!"

Dad loved that story. Every time he told it, he convulsed with laughter, repeating the punch line over and over. "Cut or shoot, motherfucker! Man, that other nigger backed off so fast. Ain't nobody in that bar was gonna mess with us then. Phil Doucette, man. That Creole bastard didn't fuckin' play! Cut or shoot!"

After the service, Dad came to New York where Good, remarried to a sweet-natured older man, had lived for several years. Philip also lived in New York, and there was someone he was eager for his old army buddy to meet.

They were radically different people. Joyce Marie Doucette was bashful and guileless, with smooth, round features and a very light complexion—"a high yellow gal," folks down South called her. A devout Roman Catholic, she attended Mass several times a week. Jake "Billy" Lamar was ambitious and extroverted, a lean, dark go-getter who believed completely in himself but in little else—certainly not in God. Even as a child I had to wonder what it was that brought them together. Maybe it was that they somehow fit into each other's plans. Maybe you grow up nursing a tangle of vague notions about what you want to do or what you are meant to do or what others tell you you are supposed to do and this mishmash coalesces into a sort of life's scheme. Over the years you are tossed and buffeted by chance happenings, accidental encounters, the whims of people who hold some measure of control over your life and your own ephemeral impulses and incessant yearnings and you struggle to give some sort of shape and coherence to experience, to find evidence that between fate or God or dumb luck, and that sketchy game plan in your mind, you have been set on some correct, inevitable course. And maybe the day arrives when you think you *should* be married, that now is the time. Suddenly someone who blundered haphazardly into your world becomes an agent of destiny. You realize—perhaps with the force of epiphany, more likely with the deceptive clarity of deliberate calculation—that this is *the one.* You see how so many of this person's qualities correspond with your life's plan. Those that do not, you try to force into conformity with your design; or you ignore them altogether, seeing only what you wish to see, for as long as you possibly can. You tell yourself this is the right person. You *know* this is the right person. Well, at least you have a pretty good hunch. "I guess," my mother once said to me, searching for a rationale, "I was in love with your daddy."

Joyce wanted desperately to build a happy family. That was her plan. She was five when her mother died of diabetes, leaving behind six children. Her father remarried and with his new wife gave Joyce nine more siblings. Joyce was sent to live with her mother's mother in Opelousas, Louisiana. But her grandmother died when Joyce was thirteen and she was sent away again, this time to New York, to live with her mother's sister Lucille. Ten years later, she was still living with Aunt Lucille, and working as a secretary, when her big brother Philip introduced her to a friend of his from the army.

Their dates were sporadic, but memorable. Billy showed Joyce a New York she'd never seen. They dined at fancy restaurants, saw shows at Radio City Music Hall, listened to the great bands that played Birdland. She had never known anyone as bright or as driven as Billy. He worked a variety of jobs—including grueling stints as a hardhat—to put himself through New York University Business School. Handsome and thoughtful, he seemed the very model of the good provider, a perfect catch. Maybe he's the one, Joyce wondered, maybe now is the time. After all, she was twenty-three and most of her girlfriends were already married. But Joyce tried not to get her hopes up. She suspected Billy was dating other women but didn't want to ask. She wasn't even sure how to define her relationship with him. They didn't see each other enough to be "going steady." Or did they? The etiquette of courtship baffled Joyce. "Before I met your daddy," Mom would tell me, "I'd never really had a boyfriend before."

Strolling through a posh section of Manhattan one evening, Billy and Joyce stopped in front of a darkened store window. Joyce fixed her eyes on a fashionably cut brown suit. "You like it, don't you?" Billy asked. "I sure do," Joyce said, "but who could afford it?" They walked on.

Weeks passed without a call from Billy. Joyce resigned herself to the idea that he was involved with another woman. "Probably some college girl," she thought. Joyce hadn't had the chance to go to college herself and regarded most of the women graduates she knew as snobs. Then one afternoon a delivery man showed up at Aunt Lucille's apartment with a beautifully wrapped package. Joyce caught her breath when she opened it and saw that expensive brown suit.

There is an ineffable sweetness about a woman who does not ordinarily consider herself pretty but who, on a certain night, just knows she's looking fine. That's how I imagine my mother, sporting her new suit, on her next date with my father.

During dinner at another stylish restaurant, Billy

leaned closer to Joyce and said he had a problem. "You see, there's this girl I like and . . ."

Joyce was stung. Of course, there was some other woman. How could she have thought Billy would choose her? What a fool she had been.

". . . and I want to propose to her," he continued, "but I just don't know how to do it. I don't know what she'll say."

Forcing a smile, Joyce said, "Just ask her, Will you marry me?"

"Just like that?" Billy said.

"Yes."

"Will you marry me?"

"That's right, just say it straight out, just like that."

"No, Joyce. Will *you* marry me?"

Once the initial shock passed, she managed to say yes.

Joyce would have fit perfectly into Billy's design. Mild-mannered, sensible, attractive and clearly very taken with him, she was the proper woman to raise his heirs while he set about amassing wealth and power. And, like Joyce, Billy wanted to create a happy, stable family. "I am determined to be a better father to my children than my father was to me," he said. Joyce was touched by that.

After a short break to go and refill his glass of scotch, my father returned to my bedroom to continue his stories. I remember thinking that chilly April day that this was a good time in our relationship. I didn't know why he'd seemed to take a greater interest in me in the past eighteen months. Perhaps it was because I'd reached the same age Dad was when his father dropped out of his life. Whatever the reason, I was flattered every time he sat down to talk.

My father was talking now of rustic boyhood days, of

hunting possum amid the Georgia pines, of sneaking drinks of corn liquor down by the river. He talked of George Brown, the husband of Good's older sister and a surrogate father of sorts, who taught him how to hunt and fish and hold his liquor. Stories I'd heard before. But there was an edge to Dad's sentimental recollections that Sunday afternoon, something beyond the usual self-aggrandizement. It was as if Dad was fascinated and terrified by his own life, as if the whole trajectory of his story seemed somehow more preposterous than glorious to him. "I'm not *supposed* to be here," he said again, shaking his head. "Me—a po' li'l ole country boy from Shingley, Georgia, an escapee from the garbage can, doing the work I do, making the kind of money I'm making. Sheeeeet. Back in Shingley, they don't even know what the fuck a financial consultant is!"

I was too embarrassed to tell Dad that I was not entirely sure what the fuck a financial consultant was either. When my father explained the complexities of the deals he worked on, I either tuned out or failed to grasp what he was talking about. I'd just nod along, hoping my father wouldn't realize what I had known for some time: that I had absolutely no interest in business.

Dad paused to take a sip of his drink and I felt compelled to fill the silence. I thought of the summer I was ten years old, when my family visited the South. I saw the farms, the small towns and dirt roads and ramshackle houses that my parents had known as children. I met aunts and uncles I never knew existed. I was fascinated to see my features, and those of my parents and siblings, reflected in the faces of my Southern relatives. I enjoyed hearing their stories about Mom and Dad as children. At first, my Southern cousins and I had approached each other tentatively. I was a skinny, nerdy kid, and my cousins' knowledge of sports and cars made me feel even more like an egghead. They pronounced New Orleans as "Nawlins" and made fun of me for saying "New Or-LEENS." I was stunned when I had to explain to a teenage cousin what a pediatrician was. In time we grew more comfortable with each other and I came to feel a strong connection to the people and places down South. But I also recognized for the first time how different I was from my parents, what strikingly dissimilar worlds we had grown up in.

"It's a long way from Shingley to New York City," I said as my father sipped his scotch.

"You damn right," Dad said.

"I guess you were pretty lucky." Even as the words left my lips, I regretted them.

Dad stared steadily at me with an expression that said, Damn, how did I ever raise such an imbecile? "It wasn't *luck*," he said mockingly. "I don't believe in luck. You *make* your luck. You follow me?"

"Uh-huh."

"It's brains and bread that get you over in this world. Not luck. You can't spend your life sittin' around waiting to get lucky. You understand me?"

"I understand."

"Ain't nobody ever became a success by relying on luck. Success is earned. You gotta work for it. You gotta make yourself a success. You gotta do it by force of will. You may come from the garbage can, but you can't act like you do. You understand what I'm saying? When I go into a meeting with these white folks to consult them on how to run their business, I can't act like some coon from Shingley, Georgia. You see, man, you have to command respect. They gotta respect you the minute you walk into the room. Which means you've got to look right. First impression is key. And you know what the most important thing is in making a first impression, don't you?"

"What?"

"Your shoes."

"Shoes?"

"Your shoes. Your shoes have got to have a fresh shine on them. That's one of the first things they're gonna notice. Why you think you see me spending so much time shining my shoes in the morning? I won't even trust them to anybody else. Shit, nobody's gonna do a better job on 'em than me. Man, I was out on the streets shinin' shoes for a nickel when I was five years old. And I made more money than all the other shoeshine boys 'cause I knew how to make those motherfuckers gleam."

I wondered nervously what my father thought of the battered, grimy white sneakers I wore all year-round.

"You gotta sweat those details, man," my father continued, his voice rising. "This is what black folks don't want to understand. Yes, a black man has to work twice as hard to get half the credit. That's just reality. That is the nit of the grit. Niggers talkin' about black power one minute then turn around whining about how 'Whitey did this to me' and 'Whitey did that' and they've got no fucking understanding of what real black power is—and what you've gotta do to go out and *get* some of that power. You gotta get what the white folks got. Show 'em you're just as good—better!—than they are. But you hear niggers talkin' about how they don't want to deal with the white man, don't want to sell out, don't want to assimilate. They want black power and they don't even fuckin' know, can't even see the facts staring them in the face, can't deal with the nit of the grit." Dad shook his head, took another sip of his drink. "*I* understand power."

CHAPTER 3

MY FIRST HOME was the St. Mary's housing project in the South Bronx. Memories of that time are cloudy, fragmented. I remember the project's criss-crossing asphalt walkways, divided by little plots of grass, and the sound of kids' roller skates scraping along the paths. I remember watching little girls jumping rope, their pigtails abounce, skinny brown legs springing with uncanny grace. I remember the lobby of our building, where it was often half dark because the lightbulbs were blown out, and people's voices echoed gratingly off the yellow, institutional walls. The walls of the elevator were all metal, the color of tin foil, and felt slick and scaly when you leaned against them. The elevator broke down a lot. It often seemed to happen when Mom and I were coming home from the supermarket and she would have to lug the bags of groceries up the fourteen flights of stairs to our apartment, cursing under her breath the whole way. Even worse was the time my mother and I were actually in the elevator when it broke down and I had my first taste of claustrophobia, standing there, trapped in the darkened car, staring up at the little rectangular window in the elevator door, frightened by the sight of the shadowy concrete ledge between floors.

And I remember driving home from the hospital, when I couldn't stop sneaking peeks at the new arrival, reaching up to my mother's lap and brushing aside the blanket to peer at his squinched, dark, tiny head. "This is your little brother Bertrand," Mom said. "Say hi to your little brother." Everybody in the car laughed when I called him "the baby." "You're just a baby yourself," said my sister Felicia, who was all of seven and a half. She was the prettiest little girl in the world—everybody said so. Lish taught me how to draw and how not to cross over the outlines when coloring in my coloring book. She devised elaborate games for us, making up TV sitcoms where we played all the characters. Soon enough, I would learn what Lish had known for nearly three years: a little brother would do anything. Eat a booger, pee in the bathtub, throw an egg out the window. All you had to do was *tell him to do it.* Little brothers were fun.

Racial consciousness was aroused at age three. Uncle Frank, Mom's younger brother, was visiting (my mother's older brother Philip, the matchmaker, would die in a car accident years before I was born). Frank worked as a groundskeeper at the projects and he often dropped by for lunch. He was a big, gregarious man with chestnut-colored skin and I got a kick out of how rugged and official he looked in his green cap and uniform. One afternoon as we sat around the kitchen table, Mom feeding Bert in his high chair, Uncle Frank complained about how obnoxious white people were.

"But Mommy's white," I said. Frank exploded in laughter. Mom just smiled and shook her head. "What's so funny?" I asked.

"Your mother ain't white," Uncle Frank said. "She's just light-skinned."

Still not comprehending, I turned to Mom. "I thought me and Daddy and Bert are black and you and Lish are white."

"No, Jakie," my mother said in a patient, explanatory tone. "We're black too. Uncle Frank and me are Creole. We had a lot of white ancestors. I have a lot of white blood in me so my skin is lighter than yours and Daddy's. Felicia takes after me so she's light-skinned too. But we're still colored people. We're all Negroes."

I had to mull that one over. I didn't know what ancestors were but I was too embarrassed to ask. Mom and Lish were black but looked white. Black and white then meant something beyond pigmentation—an idea that had never entered my mind—but what it meant exactly I didn't know. Something having to do with blood. And so my first encounter with racial awareness was at once enlightening and confusing, and shot through with ambiguity. The pattern had been set.

Most men are neither good fathers nor bad fathers, but rather, better or worse fathers at different times in their children's lives. When I was very young, my father was very good.

In my earliest memory of Dad, he is running into a swarm of traffic, dodging cars as horns honk and tires screech, all to retrieve my favorite cowboy hat, which the wind had blown off my head as we walked down the street together. Dashing and tumbling around the apartment with Dad, crawling under the coffee table, taking cover behind the couch, peeking out from behind bookshelves to fire our toy six-shooters at imaginary bad guys. He was the sheriff and I was the deputy—except for those times when I was the sheriff and he was the bad guy and we'd have our big showdown and I'd draw first and fire and Daddy would clutch his heart and cry, "Ya got me!" as he crashed to the floor. My father and I watched Westerns on TV—shoot-

'em-ups, he called them. *Gunsmoke* and *Rawhide* were the best but Dad would watch anything with horses and guns in it. We liked to watch Bugs Bunny together too and sometimes Dad laughed so hard at the cartoons it looked almost as if he were crying.

Dad's mother often came to visit, always with a batch of treats in tow: glazed donuts, peppermint Lifesavers and chocolate bars, her famous, sublime fried chicken. Sitting in my grandmother's lap, I felt a special dimension of closeness between us, as if she and I shared some secret that nobody else knew. Then again, I suspect that Good had that effect on a lot of people. While my grandmother did not resemble my father in most ways, their eyes were nearly identical. Despite her air of serenity, there was a hardness in Good's eyes. My mother, Uncle Frank, most people I'd met on the Doucette side of the family, had enormous, almost perfectly round eyes that gave their faces an expression of mild surprise. But the eyes of my father and grandmother were more narrow; the eyeballs themselves seemed practically flat. Theirs were eyes that seemed always to be taking the measure of people; eyes full of intelligence, skepticism, cunning.

Dad was smart; that was what grown-ups constantly told me. And being smart, I gleaned, was just about the most important thing in life. People were always visiting, coming by for dinner or poker games with Dad. My father was invariably the focus of any group; even in a large gathering of people, whenever a guest had a comment to make, they seemed to address it to Dad. There was lots of laughter in the house. My grandmother said that when two Lamars ran into each other on the street, they immediately broke into giggles: "Don't even say hello. Just start laughing." It was a house full of music: Ray Charles, Nat King Cole,

Dionne Warwick, Cannonball Adderley, Count Basie, Sarah
Vaughan, all the great Motown acts, James Brown, Aretha
Franklin, the Beatles. And books: books stacked high on
shelves, piled on the dining table and Dad's nightstand, big,
fat books with teeny letters and drawings of triangles and
arrows and jumbles of numbers. When I was four and able
to understand where my sister disappeared to for several
hours each weekday—when I learned that she actually got
to go to school and read books—I was sick with envy, incon-
solable until Mom went out and bought me a Snoopy bookbag of my own so that every morning I could stuff my
coloring books in it and escort Mom and Lish to the local
parochial school. Lish would kiss us goodbye and then
merge into the mob of other uniformed girls and boys
crowding through the doors of the red brick building. And
I'd return home with Mom; but it made me happy just
pretending to go to school.

   In the mid-sixties, my father's career began to take
off. After working as a Treasury agent and then as a teacher
of business and accounting at a community college, Dad, I
was told, had won an important new job. I had no idea
what it meant to be Director of Fiscal Management for the
Human Resources Administration—it was just a muddle
of official-sounding words to me—but I did know that
Dad was suddenly a very big deal. As treasurer of one of
the city's largest social services organizations, he talked
regularly to the mayor, John V. Lindsay (I liked that he had
the same initials as my father and me). Dad's name appeared in the newspapers. He was, people said, one of the
highest-ranking Negroes in city government. I loved it when
adults gazed down at me and said, "Ah, you must be little
Jake," honored to share the name of such an admired per-
sonage. Dad made everybody laugh one night when he told

the story of the dazzled HRA employee who came up to him and asked, "Mr. Lamar, how many brains do you have?"

My father soon left HRA to become vice president of a successful construction company, one completely owned and operated, Dad noted proudly, by Negroes. We moved out of the projects. After life at St. Mary's, our new neighborhood bore an almost epic grandeur. We lived two blocks west of the Grand Concourse, an expansive eight-lane boulevard, and two blocks east of the palatial old Yankee Stadium. Our new address, 811 Walton Avenue, was a stately prewar building with a huge courtyard that you entered through an archway, and an airy, mirror-filled, art deco lobby. Our sixth-floor apartment looked out on lush Franz Sigel Park and the regal Bronx County Courthouse. The new apartment seemed capacious compared to our home in the projects. A long hallway connected the front of the apartment—the foyer, living room, dining room and kitchen—to the back, where you found Mom and Dad's bedroom, Felicia's room and, to my astonishment, *two* bathrooms. The bedroom I shared with Bert was in the middle of the long corridor. We were only the second black family to move into the predominantly Jewish building. While folks seemed friendly enough to me, Mom complained that the neighbors were nosy: "Always wanting to know our business."

It was impossible to pinpoint when the strain began but, at six years old, I could feel it, the low-wave anger and agitation between my parents. Both Mom and Dad were slipping deeper within themselves. Fewer guests came over. We saw less and less of my father. He said he worked so long and hard that he had to spend many nights on the couch in his office. Mom didn't believe him. Yet, when he came home Dad often worked late into the night. In the morning, the dining room table was covered with the trappings of Dad: long, yellow notepads with narrow columns of numbers, a slide rule and adding machine, those pencils he liked that looked like pens—streamlined gold and silver shells with little points of lead poking out of the tips—and the squat, empty glass (when you put your nose to the rim and sniffed, the sharp smell burned your nostrils).

Mom hated waking Dad for work, so she assigned the task to me. Dad was a slow riser. Half an hour after you'd first nudged him awake, a full hour after he'd reached up and turned off the buzzing alarm clock, you would find him sitting hunched over on the edge of the bed, staring, bleary-eyed, into space. He looked so sad and weary, as if he were trying to muster the strength to go out and face the world again.

Sometimes when he got home after everyone else had gone to bed, Dad would fall asleep in the living room, fully clothed, in front of the television. One night after I woke up to go to the bathroom, I tiptoed to the living room and found him slumped on the couch, his head tilted back. His loud, rumbling snore sounded like some vile beast trapped inside his head, choking, snorting, struggling to get out. On the black-and-white TV people in old-style hats and coats talked rapidly at each other. I crept toward Dad. Kneeling beside him on the couch, I saw that his glasses were twisted almost sideways on his face. His thin lips were curled back and quivered slightly with each snore. I peered into his mouth. I saw a little canal of bubbly saliva between his lower lip and gum. There, just below the bottom row of teeth, were little slats of wood: a toothpick broken in four pieces, or perhaps two toothpicks, each bitten in half. Suddenly, I had an image of Dad swallowing one of those splinters and strangling in his sleep. I wanted to wake him, but I feared he might jump up and inadvertently gulp down a piece of toothpick and choke to death. I felt that Dad's life was in my hands. The beast inside his head gurgled malevolently. Slowly, gingerly, I reached into his mouth and, with thumb and forefinger, removed a splinter. The beast stirred. Holding my breath, I plucked the three remaining wood chips from his mouth. Mission accomplished, I left Dad snoring obliviously on the couch. For some reason, I did not wish to wake him. I returned to bed feeling proud, heroic, certain that I had just saved Daddy's life.

My father started yelling a lot. If he came home late and dinner wasn't waiting for him on the table, he yelled at my mother. If, when he got up in the morning, the temperature of the bath my mother had run for him wasn't just right, he yelled. He yelled at Mom that she made his fried eggs too greasy, so every morning she had to carefully pat them dry with a paper towel.

Mom was always busy—cleaning the house, doing the shopping, preparing the meals—and the tasks seemed to take more and more out of her. She was often ill, with asthma, gastritis, severe headaches. But it was my mother's emotional fragility that I sensed most acutely. Sorrow surrounded my mother like an invisible force field. Some part of her, I felt, was becoming inaccessible to us; we could not break through the sorrow to reach it. Mom took Bert and me to the Museum of Natural History one Saturday. We moved silently through the exhibits. Later, standing on the subway platform to catch the train back to the Bronx, Mom started to cry. Bert and I kept asking what was wrong, but she wouldn't tell us. That night Mom sat on the floor while Felicia braided her hair. Her hands played nervously in her lap. "Sometimes," my mother said, "I wish I were a little girl." Her voice disturbed me; it sounded like it was coming from someplace very far away.

Something like a memory, something like a dream, the scene resurfaces from time to time, hazy and chaotic. I hear the sounds first, the shattering of glass and the scream. I see the living room of our old apartment in the projects; the room is full of people, men in suits, women in nice dresses. I see my mother sitting on the couch, weeping hysterically, holding her hand to her face. Yellowish liquid is splattered on the white wall behind her head. Daddy stands across the room, yelling and pointing at her. Movement and darkness. Is someone carrying me? Covering my eyes? I am in my bed now, shaking all over. A woman's voice speaks soothingly to me. It is not my mother's voice; nor my grandmother's. Is it an aunt? One of my parents' friends? I can smell her sweet perfume and hear her bracelets jangling softly in the dark. "Shhh. Go back to sleep now, Jakie," the lady whispers, gently stroking my head. "Go back to sleep."

Every weekday morning, I donned my uniform: the white shirt and plaid tie, the gray pants, the black shoes and blue blazer with the school insignia stitched on the breast pocket. Walking through the schoolhouse doors, I could feel my stomach muscles tightening. The summer before I began Catholic school, I had already developed a profound terror of nuns. For months, Felicia had regaled me with stories of black-clad disciplinarians brutalizing children with sadistic glee. Yet, on my first day of school, my teacher Sister Margaret turned out to be not the evil crone I'd imagined but an unnervingly ebullient would-be Mary Poppins who brought a turntable to class, put on "Getting to Know You" from *The King and I* and proceeded to lip-synch the song, dancing up and down the aisles of the classroom, her inky habit billowing and twirling as she cavorted, swooping down to put her bright pink face close to yours and flashing a megawatt smile, then spinning away again as the lady on the record sang, "Getting to know youuu, getting to feel free and eeeazeeee . . ."

But Sister Margaret soon turned tough, solemnly threatening one day that any student who scored below a seventy-five on the next arithmetic test would be struck on the knuckles with a ruler. Nearly everyone failed the exam. Sister Margaret started at the back of the classroom. As she moved down the aisle I heard her say to each pupil, "Hold out your hand"—then, the sudden crack of heavy wood on bone. When my turn came, the smack of the ruler was even more painful than I'd anticipated. But that wasn't why I found myself fighting back tears; it was the shame of failure that hurt so much. This was the first and last time I would perform poorly on a test in parochial school.

The school I attended had a fairly even mix of black, Hispanic, Irish and Italian students, and a handful of Asians. While the nuns preached tolerance, many kids, no doubt parroting what they heard at home, taunted each other with ethnic epithets. Generally, though, a kid had to prove to be somehow uncool before he got hit with slurs. So I was far more worried about being considered a teacher's pet than called a nigger. One year, as the best male student in my class, I was made to sit at the head of the boys' row. Beside me, at the head of the girls' row sat a quiet Asian girl who kids routinely called "Edna the chink." I often wondered how she could stand the teasing.

Though I had, since the first grade, developed an excruciating shyness, I tried to be friendly to all the other students, hoping my congeniality would preempt any harassment.

I maintained simultaneous crushes on two girls, Alexandra and Eileen. Alex was a chubby-cheeked girl with big, doll-like eyes and skin that made me think of Hershey's Kisses. I displayed my affection by tugging on her pigtails in the playground, then running away. Occasionally, I got up the nerve to tell her a knock-knock joke. Eileen was a red-haired, freckle-faced Irish girl with an overbite, bookish like me. On those rare occasions when I mustered the courage to talk to her, we both glanced at the ground and giggled a lot. It didn't occur to me that I was supposed to prefer one of these girls over the other.

I talked to God constantly. Walking to school, I prayed to do well on a test. Playing stickball in the schoolyard during recess, I prayed the ball wouldn't be hit my way, knowing I was too clumsy to catch it. I prayed that Alex and Eileen would like me as much as I liked them. I dutifully memorized my catechism, told the truth at confession, enjoyed the taste of Communion wafers. When I told a lie, I agonized, fearing that I would be sentenced to Hell. I had a nervous stomach and believed that my frequent bouts of diarrhea were punishment for my sins. Sitting on the toilet in the middle of the night, I apologized to God for all the bad things I'd done and asked him to please take the pain away. I believed in guardian angels—winged, haloed protectors from Heaven who watched over us mortals, keeping us out of danger, guiding us in the right direction. I considered becoming a priest when I grew up.

Sunday mornings, Mom took Lish and Bert and me to Mass; my father stayed home and slept late. Dad made fun of Mom for believing in God. At holiday dinners when Mom suggested we say grace, Dad called out "Grace!" as if he were summoning a woman by that name. "You said to say Grace," he'd shrug, winking at me, "so I said it."

Jehovah's Witnesses sometimes rang our doorbell, promoting their religious literature and its message of salvation. If one of us kids answered the door, Mom had us politely get rid of the canvasser by telling him we were a Catholic family and not interested in joining any other religion. But one afternoon, when a Jehovah's Witness showed up, it was Dad who answered the door. My father cheerfully welcomed the haggard, frail-looking black man into our apartment, sitting him down at the dining room table. Encouraged by such hospitality, the man spoke enthusiastically about his faith. Daddy nodded and thumbed through a copy of *The Watchtower.*

"Well, I'll tell you, man," Dad said, "I'm a Lamarist."

"I beg your pardon?" the Jehovah's Witness asked.

"I'm a Lamarist."

"Uh, I'm afraid I'm not familiar with that sect."

"You mean you don't *know* about Lamarism?"

"No sir."

"Well," my father said, his voice rising, "I believe in the power of Jake Lamar. And this is my God." Dad took a twenty dollar bill out of his wallet and held it aloft. "I pray to the almighty dollar!" He slammed the bill down on the table, clasped his hands, bowed his head, and intoned: "Holy! Holy! Holy! O holy money!"

Discombobulated, the Jehovah's Witness quickly gathered up his magazines and rushed out the door. Devout as I was, I still had to laugh at Dad's outrageous stunt. Weeks later, my father ran into the man on the elevator. "So," my father said, grinning insouciantly, "when are you gonna come by for some more religious instruction?" The elevator stopped at the third floor and the Jehovah's Witness hurried out. "Y'all should *all* be Lamarists," Dad called after him, "and quit wasting your time with this Jesus crap!"

Despite his contempt for religion, Dad made it clear that we were expected to excel at parochial school. One Saturday night when I was in the third grade, my father took the family out to a Japanese restaurant. I mentioned casually that I'd soon be learning about Japan in social studies. When I returned from church the next morning, I found Dad sitting at the dining room table with an encyclopedia. He instructed me to read everything in it about Japan. The pages were long, with dense columns of tiny print that seemed to go on and on. I read all day. That evening Dad gave me a written test with forty questions. He was irritated when I only answered about thirty correctly. The next day, the teacher announced we would be skipping the Japan chapter in our textbook and studying China instead. Dreading another home examination, I decided not to inform my father.

Dad taught me to play chess, but he never allowed me to win. He checkmated me, then showed me what I did wrong and how he was able to take advantage of my mistakes. My father didn't expect me to beat him, but he wanted me to do everything I could to win. Anything less than total effort disgusted him. I became the competitor Dad wanted me to be. I did well in school and flaunted my success before my brother and sister, whose grades weren't as high as mine. As much as anything, it was fear that motivated me. Fear of nuns, of course, but an even greater fear that if I didn't compete, if I didn't win, my father would somehow stop loving me. Fear of losing Dad's affection, combined with his increasing absence from the apartment and his anger toward my mother, became fear of Dad himself. At nine years old, I was terrified of my father.

I grew up watching the sixties on TV. My very earliest memory was of my mother crying as we watched President Kennedy's funeral. With my nose inches away from the flickering screen, I puzzled over how newsmen could calmly give their reports from the jungles of Vietnam while a firefight raged behind them. I watched, more in mystification than in horror, white policemen on horseback charging into a crowd of black people on the Edmund Pettus Bridge. I watched ghettos burning to the ground.

My mother explained the civil rights movement to me, teaching me about Martin Luther King and Rosa Parks and Medgar Evers, telling me of the evils of prejudice and segregation. I came to understand that the world was in the midst of great change. I could see it in our own neighborhood, which was rapidly growing more integrated. While I noticed the increasing number of black families moving into the area, somehow it didn't register with me that all of the families moving out were white. "White flight" was not yet a part of my vocabulary. I simply felt lucky to live in an area where black and white people seemed to get along.

Mom started buying more African art for the house, statuettes of noble-looking black women, masks to be hung beside the conventional American landscapes and still lifes that decorated our walls. My father was indifferent to such gestures. Dad simply told me that if I worked hard and excelled in school, no one would care about my race. Dad abhorred radical activists like Stokely Carmichael and Angela Davis. He mocked people who wore afros and dashikis. A registered Republican, he would end up voting for Richard Nixon in three presidential races. In 1969, at a Fourth of July cookout for the construction firm's executives and their families, Dad sat in a circle with his colleagues as they debated whether to identify their company as "black" or "Negro." My father's basic argument was "What difference does it make?"

My parents forbade us to watch *The Little Rascals*, TV reruns of the *Our Gang* movie series from the thirties and forties. They remembered the serial all too well from their own childhoods. Dad especially could not stand the sight of Buckwheat, the wild-haired, bug-eyed pickaninny who served as the butt of the show's racist humor. "My kids aren't gonna grow up watching that crap," my father said. I began to notice the dearth of black people on television. I was struck by a soda commercial showing scantily clad white women and robust young white men frolicking in the sand and surf while a pseudo–Beach Boys tune played on the soundtrack. I wondered vaguely where people like me fit into such a world—or if we did at all. I was riveted to the positive black images that did appear on the screen: Bill Cosby as the wry secret agent on *I Spy*; Greg Morris as the electronics whiz on *Mission: Impossible*; Diahann Carroll as the beautiful widowed nurse in *Julia*; and Sidney Poitier— gorgeous, dashing Sidney Poitier, fairly oozing dignity and righteousness—in any role he played. After Daddy and Dr. King, Poitier was my biggest hero.

For all my parents' talk of racial equality, they sometimes sounded prejudiced themselves. I flinched when I heard them tell ethnic jokes in which black people were cast as liars and fools. Dad complained about "ignorant niggers" and "niggerish behavior." Mom would occasionally let slip a comment about "loud, nappy-headed women who don't know how to act." Despite having "good hair," my mother still regularly applied the straightening comb to her head. It was a gruesome-looking instrument, a row of heavy, black metal teeth with a black wooden handle. Mom heated up the comb by placing it directly on top of one of the stove burners. Engulfed in blue flames, the metal emitted an acrid, oily smell. I couldn't understand why Mom didn't cry out in pain when she ran the straightening comb through her hair. Dad, meanwhile, needled my mother by ogling white women on the street or on television. "If she's white, she's right," he'd say with a leer.

I often heard Mom talking on the telephone with friends and relatives, damning my father and all the men of her race. Black men were selfish. Black men were cruel. Black men would screw any woman with a pulse—especially if she was white. "You know, Mom," I said one afternoon, "when I grow up, I'm gonna be a black man. Are you going to hate me then too?" She gave me an impatient look. "Well," she said shortly, "you'll just have to be different." From then on, when Mom complained to women in her family, she spoke in Creole patois so I wouldn't understand what she was saying. But I knew that each day her bitterness deepened.

I hear the click of the key in the lock and snap awake. I hear the heavy footsteps, the gravelly sigh, the rustle as he takes off his trenchcoat. I sense that Bert too, lying in his bed on the other side of the room, is wide awake now. Waiting. I check the clock at my bedside: one-thirty. I drift back into a woozy half sleep.

"I said get your fat ass outta the bed and fix me some dinner, woman!"

The voice is thunderous and so thick with theatrical

bombast that I wonder at first if he's joking. Sometimes, he just taunts her briefly, letting off steam, and it's all over in a few minutes. I wait for the next explosion, the confirmation that this will be another fight night.

"You heard me, woman! Get off your fat ass!"

Bert is out of bed in an instant. I see the whiteness of his pajamas through the dark; he stands poised near the door of our bedroom. Mom's voice is muffled but I can catch the tone. She's talking low, the words coming out fast through clenched teeth. Suddenly, another explosion. "Don't gimme that shit, you fat black bitch!"

Bert takes off, leaving the door open behind him. Light from the hallway pours into the bedroom. Mom is screaming now. "I'm sick a you comin' in here all hours of the night tellin' me what to do! I'm sick of it!"

Please stop please just stop please please be quiet. Maybe if I tell them I have a math test in the morning, they'll stop. Or at least fight more quietly.

I hear Bert's voice now, high-pitched and quivery. "Come on, Daddy, let's go to bed now." He's trying to sound casual, trying to get Dad to smile. "Come on, Daddy. You're tired. Let's go to bed." I can picture him, small and chubby in his pajamas, reaching up and tugging on my father's arm. "Come on, Daddy, kiss and make up." Doesn't he know by now it won't do any good? They just keep yelling over Bert's head.

"Get your fat ass outta the bed and cook me some damn food!"

"I ain't cookin' you nothin', nigger! I'm trying to get some sleep!"

"Sleep! All you do all fuckin' day long is sleep! You know damn well you don't do nothin' but lie around in the fuckin' bed all day!"

"Aw, come on, Daddy—"

"Bert!" I hear Mom say, as if noticing him for the first time. "Get on back to bed."

"You heard me, woman! Get up and make my goddamned dinner!"

"Make it yourself!"

I shut my eyes tight, put the pillow over my head. *Please God let them stop. I have a test in long division tomorrow morning.* I hear footsteps in the hall, hear him striding past my bedroom. *Maybe it will be quiet now. Maybe it's over now. Thank you, God.*

"Jakie." Bert's voice comes from the foot of the bed. "Jakie. Jakie, I know you're awake." He shakes my leg. "Jakie, get up."

I sit up and face him, trying to look and sound as if I've just awakened. "What?"

I hear Dad in the kitchen now, slamming pots and pans. I hear the refrigerator door swing open and bang against the wall, rattling jars and bottles. He turns on the tap at full force. The rusty pipes whine. From the master bedroom on the other side of the apartment, Mom yells: "Goddamnit, shut up!"

"You have to get up, Jakie," Bert says.

"What good will it do?" I ask. "Just let them get it all out. Maybe it'll be over soon."

Felicia walks in, wearing a red nightshirt, her hair in braids. "You better get up, Jakie," she says. Her voice is even, her face impassive. "We've got to do something."

Mom's shadow passes quickly in the doorway.

"It never does any good," I say. "Just let them work it out."

"Pick that up!" Mom screams. Her voice, reverberating off the kitchen walls, gives us a start. "You pick that up, nigger!"

"Shut the fuck up!" Dad spits out the words.

"Well, you can stay here if you're scared," Felicia says. She walks across the room and grabs my brother's baseball bat. "Let's go, Bert."

They leave. I sit in bed with my knees up, my hands folded at my ankles. A pot crashes in the sink. *You can't let this get to you. You can not let it get to you. You just have to be tough. You can't let this get to you.*

"I swear to God," Mom says, her voice cracking, "I swear I'm gonna kill you someday."

"You wanna kill me? You come and try to kill me, bitch. Please do. Please do!"

Bert runs back in. "Come on, Jakie, we need you." I stumble into the hall; the light stings my eyes. Felicia stands at the end of the hallway, the bat slung over her shoulder. "Let's go," she says. But Lish does not take the bat with her, leaving it in the hall instead.

As we turn to enter the kitchen, Dad storms out, walking right past us as if we weren't there. He walks into the dining room, slams a bowl of warmed-over gumbo on the table and sits down. He still has his vest and tie on. As Bert and Lish and I stand watching dumbly, Dad attacks the gumbo, slurping the broth and staring into the bowl. He lifts a chicken leg out of the bowl and bites into it. I watch his jaw muscles working as he chews; his left temple, glistening with sweat, pulsates with each bite. Through the kitchen doorway, I see Mom, wearing her yellow nightgown, her hair tousled, slowly picking things up and putting them back in cabinets and the refrigerator.

"Woman," Dad barks, "fix me a drink."

Mom comes out of the kitchen. "Y'all go on back to bed now," she says wearily. Bert and I look to Lish to make the first move. She stares silently at my mother. "You do what I say, Lish. Get on back to bed."

"You heard me, woman," Dad says, his mouth full of food. "Fix me a drink."

"Fix it yourself," Mom snaps.

Dad rips the last piece of meat off the chicken leg and, with deliberate nonchalance, tosses the bone on the floor. "Pick that up," Mom says, her voice breaking again. Dad ignores her. With the back of his hand, he knocks the bowl off the table, spilling the brown broth, rice, okra and sausage on the carpet. "I've had enough of you!" Mom shouts. "I can't take this anymore!"

My father rises and places his palms flat on the table. Leaning forward, almost smiling, he says, "Go fuck yourself."

Mom moves toward him. "Don't you talk to me like that."

"Go—fuck—your—self!" Dad yells, pronouncing each syllable grandiosely. "Go—fuck—your—self!"

"Don't you talk to me like that in front of these children!"

"Go—fuck—your—self!" Dad says, walking away from the table, drawling extravagantly. "Go—fuck—your—self!"

"Shut up!" Mom cries. "Shut up shut up shut up shut up!"

Suddenly, Dad grabs a vase from the credenza—the round, green glass vase. He raises it above his head.

"Daddy, no!" somebody screams.

Dad hurls the vase to the floor. It shatters on the carpet.

Silence.

Mom puts her hand to her mouth. "My vase," she says. Her voice goes small and squeaky like a little girl's. "You broke my anniversary vase." She closes her eyes and the tears start to roll down her cheeks. "You broke my anniversary vase," she sobs. "You broke my anniversary vase."

Nobody moves. Mom stands alone crying. My brother, my sister and I stare at the vase, now smashed into a dozen shimmering green shards. We had saved up from our allowances to buy it for Mom and Dad's anniversary the year before. Dad stands with his chest flung out, his head tilted back. His face looks so strange, almost as if he's wearing a mask. At first, he looks cocky, proud of what he's done; then bemused, as if this were all rather entertaining. He turns and lifts another vase from the credenza.

"Don't!" Felicia cries.

He throws it down, but not very hard—it just rolls across the carpet, unbroken. Dad goes "Humph," and walks out of the dining room. He disappears down the hall and, a moment later, the door to the master bedroom slams shut.

We all hug Mom and after a while she stops crying. "I'm sorry, kids," she says, wiping her eyes. "I loved your present so much." That's all right, I say, we'll buy you another vase. Maybe we can put this one back together, Lish says, I bet we could. We help Mom clean up the dining room and kitchen. Everything is back in its proper place when Dad emerges from the bedroom. He's wearing a different three-piece suit now. He smells of Old Spice and Vitalis. He goes to the foyer closet, puts on his trenchcoat and hat, picks up his briefcase and, without a word, walks out the door.

Later, as my brother and I settle into bed, Felicia comes in. She sits on Bert's bed and asks if he's all right. "Do you think he'll come home tomorrow night?" Bert asks.

"I don't know," Lish says.

"Well," I say, not knowing what to say but feeling I should say something, "I guess it could have been worse."

"Oh, yeah?" Lish says. "You don't care."

"I do so."

"Do not." She leaves, closing the door behind her. Darkness.

"Jakie?" Bert says after a while. "Jakie, are you awake?" I don't answer. "Jakie. I know you're awake."

You can't let this get to you. You can not let it get to you. You have to be tough. You can't let this get to you. You can't let this get to you.

I start running long division problems through my head.

Dr. King was assassinated the week after my seventh birthday, and for several years afterward, on nights when I lay in bed, drifting between sleep and wakefulness, I would sometimes imagine him appearing in my bedroom in his standard dark suit and narrow black tie. Dr. King would sit on the edge of my bed and speak calmly to me, telling me that if I could just hang on, everything would be all right. In the middle of one night when I was ten, Dr. King was just fading from my imagination as Bert shook my shoulder. Mom and Dad wanted to see us in their bedroom.

Mom sat on their bed in her bathrobe; Dad stood with his vest unbuttoned, his tie loosened. "Your mother and I might be separating," Dad said. "If we do, we want to know who y'all would rather live with—me or her." I felt as if I'd just had the wind knocked out of me. I had never imagined that my parents would split up. Despite all their fighting, despite my father's long stays away from home, it was impossible for me to envision life with only Mom or Dad. I couldn't make a decision. I wanted to ask if we could sleep on it, but my father stared at us with a severe expectancy, his hands on his hips. He had presented us with an either/or proposition and he wanted an answer—now. My mother stared at the floor.

"Mom," Felicia said. "I want to live with Mom."

"Jakie," my father said, "who do you want to live with?"

"Mom," I said, since that was what Lish said.

"Fine," my father said, annoyed. "Get on back to bed."

A faint, nearly imperceptible smile passed my mother's lips.

"I want you two to stay together," Bert said.

"Y'all go on back to bed," Mom said quietly.

Walking back to my bedroom, all I could think was that I wanted the fighting to stop. That was all I wanted. If separating meant an end to the fighting, then maybe a separation would be for the best. I began to hope dimly that my parents would get divorced.

Several nights later, for the first time in months, the whole family shared a Sunday dinner together. My parents teased each other playfully. Lish and Bert and I didn't even argue over whose turn it was to wash the dishes. After dinner, we all sat down to watch a television show. Dad and Mom sat on the couch holding hands; I couldn't remember the last time I'd seen them be even so mildly affectionate with each other.

The program ended and my parents disappeared into their bedroom. The telephone rang. Not a minute later, I heard my mother's scream. Dad came storming down the hall. He grabbed his hat and coat and marched out the front door. Mom had received a call from an old friend down South, a man she hadn't spoken to in ages. Because of the cheerful way she greeted the caller, Dad evidently assumed it was some secret lover. Without a warning, without a question or an accusation, he immediately snatched the telephone receiver from my mother and bashed her over the head with it. Mom would have a bluish bruise on her temple for a long time; the doctor was surprised she didn't suffer a concussion.

The night after the attack, Dad returned home, packed two suitcases and took off again. I felt relieved; at least, the fighting would stop now. I slept a bit more easily.

My mother commiserated with other women in the building. I was amazed to learn how many of these marriages had been marked by violence. There were the Marcuses, the middle-aged black couple who moved into the building the same year we did and who had seemed perfectly pleasant, if not downright bland; Bob and Judy, the pale, long-haired Jewish couple my father called "the hippies," who played "Bridge Over Troubled Water" over and over on their stereo; Monica and Joe: she was a strapping Irish woman who looked as if she could easily pummel her short, potbellied Italian husband. Yet Joe, like Mr. Marcus, like Bob, like my father, had attacked his wife. It was incomprehensible to me how a man could hit a woman. But I was equally confounded by the way my mother and her friends talked about the incidents; the weary resignation in their voices, as if the violence was something to be expected, something normal.

About a month after moving out, Dad called to say he wanted to see Bert and me on the weekend. He wanted to take us to shoot hoops at a local basketball court, something he had never done before. My brother and I didn't talk much that Saturday afternoon. As we tossed up our shots, I felt there was something suspicious and fake going on. While my father advised us on our form and complimented our shots, he seemed stiff, distracted; he didn't seem to want to be there.

My father took us home. Dad and Mom greeted each other awkwardly, then went into the living room. Bert and

Lish and I hovered near the doorway, trying to hear what they were saying, but their voices were too low. I felt certain they were working out the details of a divorce. Finally, they called us into the living room. Dad sat in an armchair; Mom was several feet away on the couch. "Well," my father said tonelessly, "I'm moving back in."

My mother nodded. "That's right," she said, her voice sounding thin and tired. "We're going to try to work out our problems."

They did not smile, they did not glance at each other. An expression I'd heard a lot lately, repeated by women on TV and my mother's friends, rang hollowly in my mind: "We stayed together for the sake of the children." I wondered if this was what my parents were doing.

CHAPTER 4

SUNDAY AFTERNOON, April 1977, sitting cross-legged on my bed, listening to the Myth of Dad. My father was on his third full glass of scotch now. I had no idea how long he had been sitting on Bert's bed talking, but it felt like a long time. He yawned and took off his glasses, bowed his head and rubbed his eyes hard. When he raised his head again, I noticed how bloodshot his eyes were. He looked around the room, his expression quizzical, as if he'd just awakened in a strange place.

"Where's your mother at?"

The question seemed innocent enough but I knew that the wrong answer could become a premise for violence. A Saturday evening a few years earlier, Dad arrived home before Mom and asked my sister where she was. Not exactly sure, Felicia gave Dad some innocuous answer: Mom was at the supermarket, or maybe the beauty parlor. Dad confronted Mom when she walked in the door. She told him the truth, that she had been out with a couple of girlfriends. Dad went wild, accusing Mom of carrying on an affair, accusing Felicia of lying to cover for her. He threw Lish around the kitchen as if she were a rag doll—fifteen years old at the time, she couldn't have weighed more than ninety pounds. "Lying is worse than stealing!" my father cried as he beat her.

So I paused for several moments that passed like several days, running through a quick calculus of the risks involved in my answer: *Do I even remember where Mom is this afternoon? Yes, I remember. Now, do I tell him the truth? What if I'm wrong? Will he think I was lying? What if I tell him I don't know—will he think I'm covering for her? What if I tell him the truth and Mom, assuming he won't believe her, walks in and tells him a lie? But what reason would Mom have to lie? Fear. That's reason enough.*

Dad leaned forward on Bert's bed, his elbows on his knees, waiting for my answer. *God, how much time has passed? Does he think I'm stalling? Tell him the truth.*

"I think she went to a bridal shower," I said quickly, "for one of her friends from the office." Pause. "Or something like that."

Dad bowed his head again, seemingly contemplating the glass of scotch on the floor between his feet. He let out a long, exasperated sigh. *Oh, shit, what's the matter? Doesn't he believe me? I told him the truth! He doesn't believe me.*

"Damn," my father hissed. "Isn't she ever home anymore?" He looked up at me. "Do you know what marriage is?"

Hell on earth seemed the obvious answer from what I had witnessed. But I didn't say that; I just shook my head.

"Marriage," Dad said slowly, "is a contract. It's *a deal.* You see, man, when your mother and I got married, we had a bargain. We had . . . an agreement. But I don't believe she remembers that. You see, your mother knew, when we got married, that I was a renegade. She knew that sometimes I'm gonna do as I please. And as long as y'all got clothes on your backs and food on the table, I am *entitled* to do as I please. Now, she may not always like that—but that was the deal!"

Dad reached down and lifted his glass, took a sip. *Am*

I supposed to say something now? Does he even want me to respond?

" 'Cause I'm a renegade," Dad said again. "I was born a renegade and I'm gonna die a renegade. See, that's how I live my life. Now, I went out a here Thursday morning. I come back today, Sunday. Now, I do not expect to get the third degree about where I been and what I been doin' for the past three days. 'Cause as long as I do for her and do for all a y'all, it ain't nobody's business if I don't come home for a few days . . . 'Cause you may not see me around here much, but when you need me . . ." Dad's voice got lower, more intense. "Hey, man, when you *need* me, I am there! I leave the day-to-day household shit, the monitoring of the nest, to the womenfolk. You dig?"

I nodded involuntarily, reflexively.

"And your mother knows that. She knows it. But it seems she no longer wants to abide by the agreement. She wants to try to challenge my authority. I come home on a Sunday afternoon and she ain't even here!"

Dad stopped suddenly. He took another sip, turned his head slightly and, looking askance, grumbled: "Women's lib."

My father was quiet for a while. I wanted to ask him what was wrong. I wanted to ask him to leave so I could get on with what I was doing. But I simply sat still, waiting for him to break the silence. Finally, he looked at me and asked, "What are you working on?"

"Nothing important," I said, reluctant to talk about myself. But then, I thought, Dad so rarely interrupted one of his monologues to ask me a question about my life, to find out what I thought about anything, I might as well seize the opportunity. "Well, not that important," I said. "It's a speech. I'm running for the student council and I have to give a speech tomorrow."

"Yeah?" Dad said, lighting up. "I did that shit. I was

president of the student body in high school *and* in college."

"I know."

"That's wonderful. Can I take a look at your speech?"

"Well, it's not done yet," I hedged. "I mean, this is just a rough draft."

"All right, man, you don't have to show me . . . Just as long as you win." The rush of anxiety I felt must have shown on my face because Dad laughed and said, "I'm only kidding." He leaned back on Bert's bed, fixing me with his appraising stare. "So—you ever think about going into politics?"

"No, Dad. I mean, not seriously anyway."

"Well, hey man," he said solemnly. "*Start* thinking about it. Do you realize that you could be president of the United States?"

I laughed.

"Don't laugh," my father said.

I stopped laughing.

"I'm serious, man. Have you ever thought that you could be president?"

"No, Dad."

"Well, you could. That's what we've got to be building for. You see, man, by the time you're my age . . . How old are you?"

"Sixteen, Daddy."

"By the time you're my age, the world will be ready for it. Why you think I've got you in that fancy prep school? So you will be prepared for your destiny. You gotta stay on the right track, though. Gotta keep gettin' those good grades. Gotta go to a top college. Now, I don't *require* that you go to Harvard, Yale or Princeton, but wherever you go, it's gotta be top-notch. You follow me?"

"Uh-huh."

"Then, on to law school. Or maybe a Rhodes Scholar-ship first. We can do it, man. It's gonna take money though. But that's why I'm out there hustlin'. Twenty-five hours a day, eight days a week. It's for you, man. For you. You know that, don't you?"

"I know."

"Nah, you don't really," Dad said quietly. "You don't really know it."

"Yes I do."

"Naw. You don't. Not yet. But you will."

Dad dreamed big. Like Nelson Rockefeller, a man Dad re-vered, my father never wanted to be *vice* president of any-thing. So, in the early seventies, he left the construction company where he had been second-in-command and started a financial consulting firm, advising the managers of small businesses. The new work proved lucrative. We ac-quired things: a large new car, expensive furniture for the living room, a color TV for the bedroom Bert and I shared. We took a vacation to Hawaii, one of the best times the five of us would ever share together. Despite his success as a financial consultant, my father still dreamed of being a cap-tain of industry, of building highways and bridges and sky-scrapers. Working with a handful of partners, he set out to establish a construction company of his own. If Mom and Dad were fighting less at night, it was because my father spent even more time away from home. But Dad provided, bountifully.

My father said he didn't give a damn if Mom wanted us to be Catholics, but he would no longer have his children attending parochial school. Felicia said she was perfectly happy to stay at her all-girls Catholic high school. But the next year, Bert and I transferred to the Ethical Culture School in Manhattan. After five years of lower middle class Catholic kids in stiff uniforms, I suddenly found myself surrounded by largely affluent, predominantly Jewish kids who wore ripped blue jeans and T-shirts to class. I was one of five minority students in my sixth-grade class of twenty-one kids, so I didn't feel whited out. What was disorienting to me was the casual self-assuredness of the Ethical students. At parochial school, I was accustomed to simply giving pat right-or-wrong answers to the sisters' questions. At Ethical, the teachers actually engaged the students in debate, asking probing questions and encouraging the pupils to challenge their statements. And the students, black and white alike, did challenge the teachers, respectfully, but without fear. They seemed to exude a sense of entitlement: they knew they were bright, their brightness was acknowledged; they had opinions and they bore no qualms about expressing them. I was, at first, intimidated by their confidence and maturity. But by the end of my first year in private school—once I realized I could hold my own against the other students academically—I too became more candid, outgoing, self-possessed.

In seventh grade, I would move on to Fieldston, the Ethical Culture School's campus in Riverdale, a suburb in the north Bronx. With its complex of buildings, grassy quadrangle and large, glass-paneled library, Fieldston resembled my image of a college more than a junior high and high school. While the student population remained overwhelmingly white and wealthy, Fieldston enrolled more black and Latino kids, many from the inner city and on scholarship, than just about any other private school in New York. It was at Fieldston, known as a "bohemian prep school," that my love of reading would breed a love of writing and my enjoyment of playacting would lead to an involvement in theater. And it was there that I made my first acquaintance with a polyphony of black voices that would help shape my way of thinking and seeing: Douglass and Du Bois, Hurston and Hughes, Hansberry and Haley and Malcolm X, Morrison and McKay, Achebe and Angelou, Brooks, Baraka, and Brown, Elder, Fuller, Toomer and Reed, Walcott and Wilson, Walker and Wideman, Shange and Soyinka, Cullen, Bontemps, Giovanni and Dove; Wright; Baldwin; Ellison.

The summer after sixth grade, my first year in private school, Dad hired tutors for me in Spanish and math so I would have an edge over other students when junior high began in the fall. Working with the tutors, I found my nervousness around adults evaporating. It was 1973 and, much to my father's chagrin, I was developing a decidedly left-of-center political consciousness. When my father said something I found politically objectionable, I'd throw up my hands and say, "Aw, come on, Dad." When he launched into one of his adamant defenses of Richard Nixon, I didn't hesitate to criticize the President for Watergate and the bombing of Cambodia. I told Dad he had been rooting for the wrong side in the cowboy-and-Indian movies he loved so much. I could detect my father's irritation at being con-tradicted but, somehow, I didn't worry about it. As I saw it, my father and I were just having lively debates.

There was nothing—no toy, no treat, no childhood privilege—that I had ever wanted as much as I wanted to grow an afro. Watching the Jackson Five on TV, Bert and I were mesmerized by Michael's enormous, fluffy helmet of hair bouncing as he bopped. We seethed with envy at the sight of schoolmates sporting 'fros the size of suburban hedges. For years, we'd begged Mom to beg Dad to please let us grow our hair long. Dad had always refused: "My sons aren't gonna look like stupid, raggedy-ass niggers." Every few weeks, Dad took Bert and me to the barber shop to have our hair cut to resemble his own: short, neat, carefully groomed with a pocket comb and Vitalis. Finally, Mom and Felicia persuaded Dad to let us grow our hair just long enough so that we could use afro picks. My father bought a home barber's kit and Lish began cutting our hair, trimming off a little less each time.

One Saturday afternoon, our eleven-year-old cousin Asa came over to hang out with Bert and me. We went to the candy store, bought a bunch of comic books and read them at the counter while drinking perfect Bronx egg creams. Leaving the store, Asa stopped to tie his sneakers. Bert and I turned the corner and hid behind a newsstand. As my cousin passed the newsstand looking bewildered, I called out, "Bye, Asa" in a goofy voice. Asa tilted his head in our direction—clearly, he'd heard me—but he didn't turn completely around. I could see him, in profile, smirking. He kept on walking. Bert and I stayed crouched behind the newsstand for a couple more minutes before we got bored. Walking the five blocks back to our house, we kept expecting Asa to jump out from behind a corner or a parked car to try to scare us. That's the way the game usually went. We arrived at the courtyard of our building; still no sign of Asa. Figuring he'd returned to the apartment, we headed upstairs.

"Where the fuck have you been!" my father screams as we walk in the door. Behind him, I see Mom and Asa sitting in the kitchen.

"We were at the candy store," I say, terrified and confused. "What's the matter?"

"What the fuck were you doin' leaving that boy alone!"

"We were just fooling around." I still don't understand what Dad is so mad about.

"Fooling around! You don't leave that boy alone by himself out in the street! What the fuck's the matter with you!"

Asa stands in the kitchen doorway, looking completely unharmed, but as stunned by my father's rage as I am.

"But Asa's fine," I say, unable to keep my voice from trembling. "He knows the way to our house."

"Don't you talk back to me!" Dad grabs me by the arm. "Anything coulda happened to that boy!"

"But he's okay!" I cry.

"Don't you talk back to me!" My father takes Bert by the arm and starts dragging both of us down the hall. "You wanna be a little smartass! I'll teach you a lesson! I'll teach you a lesson!"

Bert and I are both screaming and crying, squirming to get out of my father's grip. "We were just playing, I'm sorry, we were just playing!"

Bert begs: "Please, Daddy, no, please, Daddy!"

My father shoves us through the doorway of our bedroom. He slaps my face. I collapse on the bed, the whole left side of my head burning. "You wanna be a little smartass! Wanna be like your little smartass friends at school! I'll teach you a lesson!"

Sobbing convulsively, my stomach contracting, I fear I may vomit. Suddenly, I feel the crack of my father's belt on my thigh. The strap is slapping me everywhere: my back, my arms, my chest, my legs. Dad keeps screaming that he's going to teach me a lesson. I still can not understand why he's so mad. His anger seems so out of proportion to the sin.

"Why are you hitting me?" I cry.

My father stops, holding the belt aloft, frozen in mid-strike. "Why am I hitting you?" he yells, as if this were the most absurd question he'd ever heard. "Why am I hitting you?" He spits the words back at me. He gives me several more lashes, then goes to the other side of the room to whip Bert. He leaves, slamming the door behind him.

Just as Bert and I stop crying, my mother comes in. "Your daddy wants to see you in the kitchen."

My father waits for us with a chair placed in the center of the kitchen. The electric clippers, scissors and combs of his barber's kit have been neatly laid out on the table. "Sit down," he says to me calmly. My father shears me so closely that I will be left practically bald, unable even to run a comb through the thin layer of hair that remains. Bert weeps as he watches the buzzing clipper slice through my afro, knowing he's next.

And it occurs to me that this punishment has nothing to do with Asa at all. It is, I realize, about more things than I can comprehend; but the one thing I know it is about is power. My father is letting me know that he has all of it, and, I, at twelve, have none. Dad's authority will not be challenged. And the only thing I can do to strike back is not to cry, not to let Dad feel even stronger at the sight of my crying. So I fight back my tears, as I watch tufts of hair tumble softly off the apron tied around my neck, forming a downy black pile on the kitchen floor.

Recession. Suddenly, in 1974, there were few consulting jobs for Dad. His fledgling construction firm went under.

We were late with rent payments. Credit cards were canceled. Savings dried up. My parents were forced to request more financial aid to keep Bert and me in Fieldston. Dad sold his car. Felicia pulled out of Adelphi University after her freshman year and returned home, where she took a job to help support herself. My mother, after eighteen years as a homemaker, returned to clerical work at an accounting firm.

Though Dad still disappeared for days on end, he began spending more time at home. He was, for the most part, a somber, silent presence in the apartment. The rest of us crept about and spoke in subdued tones when he was around. My father maintained one of his habits of better times, staying up late working at the dining room table. But instead of working on the graphs and charts and reports of old, he now toiled over the *Daily Racing Form.* Dad had become obsessed with horse racing, spending long days at the local Off-Track Betting parlor and even longer nights in the dining room, trying to pick the next day's winners, employing his own peculiar, pseudo-scientific method, using a slide rule and mathematical formulas to divine the outcome of races. Dad treated gambling as a demanding, full-time job. He was exultant after his victories, coming home with bagfuls of groceries and goodies, passing out twenty dollar bills and bragging about how he orchestrated the big score.

But come the holidays, Dad hit a losing streak. There were few presents under the tree on Christmas Eve. My father didn't come home that night. He walked in drunk the next afternoon. Before he could take off his trenchcoat, Felicia handed Dad a card and wished him a Merry Christmas. Dad tore open the envelope. Two fifty dollar bills fluttered to the floor. My father stared at the money lying on the faded beige carpet. "Lish," he said hoarsely. "Daddy doesn't need your money." Tears rolled down his cheeks. He turned away from us and pressed his forehead against the wall. "Daddy doesn't need it," he murmured through his tears. "Daddy doesn't need it." He trudged slowly down the hall and disappeared into his bedroom.

At the height of our family's financial crisis, Dad was offered an executive position with a huge corporation. The job offered him a higher salary than he had ever earned and the promise of long-range financial security. My father turned it down. At forty-two, he found the idea of working for somebody else unbearable. Despite his obsession with money and our dire situation, Dad could only accept success on his own terms. Despite his belief in assimilation, the notion of working in a vast, white institution repelled him. He muttered something about not wanting to be a "corporate Uncle Tom," kowtowing to bosses to get that big raise or promotion. More than acceptance from whites, my father needed to be his own man. Dad had to possess; he had to create. He had no desire to be a CEO when he dreamed of being a tycoon. My mother, struggling to keep us solvent on her weekly paycheck, was overwrought when Dad said no to the corporation. But I secretly admired him for it.

I was in eighth grade that year and doing a lot of things for the first time: going to parties; getting drunk; smoking pot; kissing a girl, a tall, beautiful, bright-eyed girl with a big, curly afro. And, for the first time, I stopped studying hard. My grade point average plummeted. Dad, who in the past had chastised me for getting grades as low as B+, said nothing about the C+ I received in science. As his bank account had dwindled, so had his authoritarianism (Bert and I were wearing our hair quite long those days). But the disappointment in his face as he read my report card cut deeper than any of his past criticism. Guilt swelled in the pit of my stomach. It was another first, the first time in my life that I felt I had let my father down.

Later that year I was stopped by a policeman at a subway station, caught flashing another student's train pass. The cop handed me a summons. When I told Mom, she was almost as scared as I was about how Dad would react to the news. Yet, my father didn't blow up. He told me that I'd done a foolish thing, but he seemed more irritated with the police than he did with me. Dad went with me to court and argued my case before the judge: "We've got fourteen-year-olds in this city mugging and killing people, and you're going to punish my son for doing something as childish and harmless as using someone else's train pass?" The judge dismissed the case. Leaving the courthouse, I felt grateful and ashamed. I was determined to somehow repay Dad for what he had done. I wanted nothing so much as to make my father proud of me again.

Dad bounced back. He doggedly rebuilt his consulting business and started trying to launch another construction company. The money began to trickle in again. Having risen from the ashes of financial catastrophe, my father seemed more colossally self-confident than ever. But the family dynamic had changed in the two years since Dad's business had gone under. Each of us went pretty much his or her own way. My mother, especially, seemed more caught up in the world outside: her work, exercise, her friends from the office. Mom finally had a social life independent of my father and the family and the result was a new pride and assertiveness. While Mom's newfound independence clearly annoyed my father, he only griped quietly about it. Instead of battling as they did in the old days, my parents simply dealt with each other as little as possible.

This was when Dad started telling me his stories. The attention made me feel privileged. As the family became more fractured, I began to feel like Dad's only ally in the house. Listening to his tales, I could understand why he had lashed out at us in the past. Having lived a hard life, he could not help but be a hard man. Dad talked to me a bit about the early days of his marriage, how my mother's constant health problems—her intestinal ailments, migraine headaches and chronic depressions—had put a strain on him. He was working as a Treasury agent back then, and he told me of the doctors' bills he'd had to pay while trying to support a young family on a government salary. He told me how financial obligations finally forced him to quit writing his dissertation, to give up one of his most cherished ambitions: earning a doctorate in economics. But Dad was tough. He had persevered. He had prevailed. My father, I believed, saw in me the same raw elements that had made him a success in the world. Through his talks, I came to realize that he wanted to cultivate me, to teach me how to be strong. To make me more like him. I was an eager pupil.

Sunday afternoon was giving way to Sunday evening. My bedroom now was filled with orange light. "So," my father said, gesturing expansively, glass of scotch in hand, "my projections were obviously the accurate ones and we were able to close the deal the same goddamned day!"

I smiled and nodded, though I hadn't the slightest idea what Dad had been talking about for the past fifteen minutes, spacing out as I did whenever he discussed his financial transactions. I used to worry that Dad would sense how tedious and incomprehensible I found the talk of his wheeling and dealing. But I had come to see that my reactions to his stories weren't terribly important to him. It was the telling that mattered.

"Some days, I don't even go into the office," my father said, almost in a whisper, and he immediately had my full attention again. "I'll just walk around town. Thinking. I'll wander around for hours, working through some problem, planning a deal, or just thinking about . . . my life. And people might say I'm not working, I'm wasting the day. But if you're really thinking, really using your brain, shit, man, that's a full day's work. Walking around the city. Thinking."

Dad fell silent. I wanted to tell him how alike we were. I wanted to tell him about my own solitary walks around Manhattan and the Bronx, about the hours I too spent lost in thought. But I didn't tell him. I didn't think he really wanted to hear.

He downed the last of his drink. "So when's your mother getting home?"

"I don't know. She didn't say."

"Damn. I tell ya, man, this shit's gotta stop. It's gotta stop." Dad rose slowly from the bed. He wobbled slightly, took a moment to steady himself. He looked at me, grimly. "You gonna be all right, Jakie. No matter what happens. Okay? You're gonna be all right." He walked over to me and smiled. "You just leave it all to me. Deal?" He held out his hand. I smiled and shook it. "Deal!" Dad said.

Yawning languidly and scratching his back, he started to leave. He stopped in the doorway and turned to face me. "I like it when we get a chance to talk together like this."

"Me too, Daddy."

He left the bedroom and I tried to get back to work.

But before I knew it, I had dozed off, fully clothed on my bed, surrounded by books and notepads, my half-written speech at my side, dreaming of nothing.

"Answer my question!"

I open my eyes to find the bedroom dim and shadowy. When did I fall asleep? How long has it been since Dad walked out of my bedroom? Look at the clock: eight-thirty. Dad's voice booms from the kitchen.

"You heard me, woman!"

"Don't you come in here with none of your craziness tonight, Billy," Mom shoots back, " 'cause I am not in the mood."

"Where the fuck were you!"

"I'm warning you, Billy."

"You don't warn me nothin'. Where the fuck were you!"

"At a damn bridal shower, all right!"

"Don't you lie to me, woman!"

Shut up shut up for God's sake please shut up. Why do they stay together? Why do they go through this over and over and over?

Bert runs in. I'm ready to tell him to leave me alone when I get a good look at his face. I have never seen him so frightened. "Jakie, come quick."

I freeze in the kitchen doorway. My mother stands at the stove, in a floral print dress, her eyes wide with fear. A few feet in front of her stands my father, wearing only a white undershirt, white boxer shorts and black socks. He is pointing a long steak knife at my mother.

"Now you're gonna tell me the truth. Where the fuck were you?"

"I told you, Billy," my mother says, her voice shaking. "I was at a bridal shower for a girl from the office and—"

"Don't you fucking lie to me, woman!"

"I'm not lying, Billy!" my mother cries.

"You're a barefaced liar!"

"Why are you calling me a liar?"

"Why! Don't ask me why!" Dad yells, throwing out his right arm in a wide arc, slicing the air with the knife.

I walk into the center of the kitchen and stand between my parents, facing Dad. I plant one of my hands firmly in the center of his chest; the other touches the bicep of his right arm; I am startled by how tense and firm the muscle feels. Out of the corner of my eye, I see the blade of the knife glinting under the fluorescent kitchen light. "Calm down now, Dad. Just take it easy."

My father does not look at me. His bloodshot eyes are trained on my mother. "I'm tired of your lies!" he screams. "I'm tired of your fuckin' lies!"

"What lies?" my mother sobs.

"Who were you fuckin'?"

"What? Nobody, Billy."

"Liar! You're a barefaced liar!"

"Calm down now, Dad. Just calm down." I slowly push Dad a couple more feet away from Mom, trying to clear a path so she can get out of the kitchen. He does not try to push me away, but he doesn't give much ground either.

"You been fuckin' everybody behind my back! You been fuckin' men on the living room floor!"

"What are you talking about, Billy? I don't know what you're talking about!"

"Liar!"

Felicia and Bert appear. They take hold of Mom and guide her out of the kitchen, into the foyer.

My father pivots and lurches forward. I keep my grip on him. "I want you outta here, you lyin' black bitch! Pack your fuckin' bags! Get outta here, you fat piece a shit!" Dad has backed me up into the foyer now. I turn and see Mom, Lish and Bert hurrying down the hall toward my parents' bedroom. I am still holding on to my father as he screams after them: "Get—out—a—here! Get—out—a—here! Get—out—a—here!"

The bedroom door slams shut. "Just calm down, Daddy. She's going, okay, she's getting ready to leave. Just settle down now. Come on, sit down here."

I walk my father back into the kitchen. He sits down at the table, still clutching the knife, muttering angrily. "She must think I'm a fool. That woman must think that I am a goddamned fool. She been fucking everybody. Behind my back!"

In the face of madness, I struggle to find some reason. But logic snaps. It is unimaginable to me that my mother has been with another man. She doesn't even seem to enjoy the company of men. I am equally certain that Dad has cheated on Mom for years—he has practically told me as much. Leaning across the table, I ask a ridiculous question, but the only one I can think of: "Daddy, are you all right?"

"She wanna live her life her way? She wanna be in women's lib? Let her be a libber! Let her try to make it out there on her own."

"Okay, Dad. You just take it easy now. Just settle down."

"This shit has got to stop," my father says, staring at the floor and slowly shaking his head. "This shit has got to stop. It has just got to stop."

Mom, Lish and Bert enter the foyer. My mother has her raincoat on and carries a suitcase. I assume she is going to stay with her cousin Louise, a widow who lives across the street.

My father jumps up from the table. "Get—out—a—

here!" he yells, waving the knife. I rise to block him, but he does not move toward the door. He just stands in the center of the kitchen, screaming: "Get—out—a—here!" I see my mother's face through the kitchen doorway. She does not look so much frightened as disoriented; she looks as if a flashbulb has just gone off in her face. Lish and Bert guide her to the front door. "Get—out—a—here!"

The front door slams, the doorbell ringing once on impact. All energy leaves my father's body. His arms fall to his sides. The knife drops from his hand and skitters across the linoleum. He mumbles something unintelligible. I leave him standing in the kitchen.

I open the front door and see Mom walking down the long sixth-floor corridor toward the elevator, flanked by my brother and sister, struggling with the weight of her suitcase. I want to say something, to call out to her, but I cannot speak. Felicia and Bert seem to disappear, the whole corridor seems to disappear; or rather, it is transformed into a wide, dusty Louisiana road, and my mother is a small child, toddling down that road, alone. And all I know is this: everything is different now.

When I return to the kitchen, Dad is gone. I go to his bedroom and crack open the door. My father lies facedown on the bed, unconscious, snoring.

CHAPTER 5

WE DIDN'T TALK about my mother. In the weeks after Mom fled the apartment, my father never mentioned her or that night, and I lacked the courage to raise the subject. My mother lived directly across the street, sharing cousin Louise's one-bedroom apartment. When I visited Mom, I tried to pretend that everything was going to be all right, struggling to keep the conversation light, acting as if this were an ordinary situation. But my mother couldn't play along. She wanted answers from me: Did Dad expect her to move back in? Did he want a divorce? A legal separation? Had he completely lost his mind or was his violent banishment of her part of some calculated plan? Because my father enjoyed talking at me, some family members assumed I knew his motivation; but I was as much in the dark as anyone. I sometimes thought my father had been only one or two drinks away from stabbing my mother. As the months passed, it became clear that Mom would not be returning and, fearing for her life if she should, I was relieved. But as my mother sank deeper into loneliness and despair, I realized that cutting Mom off from her children was the cruelest thing my father could have done. With no other rationale evident, I wondered if cruelty itself had been the purpose.

My father became stranger than ever to me. In a mystifying break with tradition, Dad began staying home all day Sunday, every Sunday. Bert and Dad and I slipped into a routine of playing backgammon while half watching the professional basketball games that were broadcast each Sunday afternoon. (Felicia generally stayed away from home as much as possible, and eventually moved out altogether.) Sunday evenings, Dad prepared dinner, usually a baked ham or a roast chicken, always as evenly cooked as they were virtually flavorless, and a steaming heap of white rice, seasoned with nothing but margarine. Sitting at the dinner table, I babbled enthusiastically about basketball or my latest accomplishments at school and nodded eagerly at all of Dad's pronouncements, playing my designated role in the fiction of Mom's nonexistence.

I walked a tightrope, trying to be attentive to Mom without getting consumed by her sorrow, trying to stay in Dad's favor while fearing he might explode again at any moment. Fieldston became my sanctuary. When I wasn't caught up in extracurricular activities that kept me at school long after dark, I hung out with friends as late as possible, forestalling the return to my father's home. Though I was still two years away from my high school graduation, I began marking off the weeks until I would be able to escape to college. Unable to comprehend what was happening to my family, my focus became getting away. I just had to hang on until I could get away.

Three years earlier, when Mom returned to office work, my grandmother started coming over twice a week to help with the household chores and cooking. Before going to school in the morning, I liked to sit in the kitchen and talk with Good. A few weeks after Dad threw Mom out, my grandmother tried to discuss it with me.

"Oh, I'm sure it will all work out in the end," I said. "I think everybody's coping fine."

My grandmother stared at me in dry-eyed empathy. "All right, sugar," she said. "We don't have to talk about it if you don't want to."

I didn't want to. Instead my grandmother talked to me about the past. At the core of most of her anecdotes were small gestures of compassion and integrity. My grandmother never lectured or sermonized; but by simply telling me the stories of her life she was instructing me on how to make my way in the world. These quiet talks with my grandmother helped, more than anything, to keep me together after my parents split.

I thought I could never trust or feel close to my father again. Yet, the more distant I felt from Dad, the more interested he seemed to become in everything I did. Late one evening, I was talking on the kitchen phone with a friend from school. After I hung up, Dad called to me from the dining room. He sat at the table, surrounded by papers. "I heard you on the phone," he said.

"You did?"

"You're going to be in another play?"

"Yeah, I am."

"Listen, man, I don't think you should get too involved in this theater stuff. The same goes for that creative writing class you're taking. Theater and writing are all well and good but you can't indulge those pursuits that are basically entertainment to the detriment of your serious studies."

"My studies aren't suffering."

"I know that. I know that right now they aren't. But you're going to be applying to colleges soon and you shouldn't be wasting your time on bullshit."

"All right."

"I also heard you say 'stupidest' on the phone. 'Stupidest' is not a word, though a lot of stupid people think it is."

"All right."

"And you giggle too much. You sound like a faggot. Your voice is too high-pitched, you sound like you're squealing. Talk like a man. You gotta sound strong, confident. Talk like you know what you're talking about."

"Yeah, well, I don't want to sound arrogant."

"What's wrong with being arrogant? *I'm* arrogant."

Marisa was an attractive, earnest fifteen-year-old with long frizzy hair and a taste for peasant skirts and earth shoes. We'd met at a party late in my sophomore year and taken a liking to each other. Sitting on a bench in Central Park one afternoon, a month or so after we'd met, she scrunched up her face and said, "So, what's it like being black?"

It was Marisa's tone more than anything that took me by surprise. There was something smug and clinical in her voice. Noticing how her eyes narrowed and her head tilted curiously, I had the sudden, queasy feeling that Marisa regarded me as some type of anthropological specimen.

"What do you mean?" I asked.

"How do you feel about being black?" Marisa said, an edge of impatience now in her voice, as if she were being quite obvious and I was being dense. "Surely you must have thought about it."

"Yeah, I like it. I like having arms and legs too."

"What I mean to say is, you must see things from a black perspective."

"Well, of course. What other perspective would I see things from?"

"Don't get defensive. I'm just trying to understand the black experience."

"Every experience I have is a black experience. I mean, I don't have any white experiences."

Marisa shook her head in frustration. She considered herself a politically correct young woman, and she was simply asking me a politically correct question. I, in turn, felt as if Marisa was anticipating some socially edifying response from me, some answer that would conform to her notions of a generic black consciousness; and if I didn't provide the answer to fit her notions, then I somehow was not authentically black. I didn't know how I was supposed to explain my existence to her. How could I explain that being black was the most important thing in my life and, at the same time, not very important to me at all?

At sixteen, I'd never been a victim of overt racism. Sure, there had been the suspicious glances from shopkeepers who thought I was going to rob them. There was that stiff formality I perceived in some white adults, friends' parents usually, who were unaccustomed to talking to black people. But these were petty annoyances. If anything, my race had been an advantage. Among a lot of white kids, blackness conferred an instant cool; they just assumed, by virtue of my being black, that I was hipper than they were. I sensed that, to many white adults, my being black was a sort of bonus—here was a kid who was smart, friendly *and* black. What a pleasant surprise it was to them! These were attitudes born of prejudice, of course, but it was a form of prejudice that did me no ostensible harm, and I took it in stride. I thought, in fact, that by simply being myself, I was helping subvert stereotypes; that if white people saw me as an individual, their preconceived notions about all black people would fade away. The trouble, as with Marisa, was getting white people to stop abstracting you, to stop turning you into a symbol, to stop asking you to explain.

It was far easier sometimes to be with one's own kind, with people who didn't need explanations. Most of the peo-

ple I knew at school were white. Most of my friends were
white. And while I had always liked to believe there was
little difference between my relationships with white kids
and black kids, I was becoming more aware of the special
dimension of intimacy I shared with my friends of color.
There was a comfort, a knowingness, a sort of exultation
among us. We could get together and talk about the peculiar nuances and prickly ironies of our lives, sustaining each
other when things got weird by reminding ourselves that we
weren't going through this alone.

Roy, the son of an interracial couple, had been my best
friend since the seventh grade. We had a favorite park in
Riverdale where we'd sit on our favorite rock, drinking
endless cans of Coke, eating Pepperidge Farm cookies and
talking into the night. I often felt that something hadn't
really happened to me, or an idea had never really developed, until I'd told Roy about it. We talked about the in-
creasingly delicate racial equilibrium at Fieldston. Interracial friendships and dating were still common, but there was
a growing wariness between black and white students. I had
decided, in my teenage wisdom, that consciousness was a
house of rooms. In it was a certain room to which my white
friends had limited access. I could welcome them in, show
them around, describe the particular characteristics of the
place to them, but they could never fully inhabit it. My black
friends, on the other hand, knew the room, knew this corner of consciousness, thoroughly, and were perfectly at
home there. But it was a big house, and in most other
rooms, all my friends, whatever their background, could
hang together. "All I know is this," Roy said, "if there's
gonna be a war, then I want to be a neutral country, all
right? I'm Switzerland."

The subtle racial tension at Fieldston turned blatant

and ugly when Tim Walker was accepted at Brown University. Tim, two years ahead of me at Fieldston, was a bright, personable middle-class black guy with an array of impressive extracurricular activities but a less than spectacular grade point average and Scholastic Aptitude Test scores. Tim's friend Jonathan was a bright, personable white guy, financially better off than Tim, who also sported interesting extracurriculars but a higher GPA and SAT scores. Jonathan was infuriated when Brown rejected him but admitted Tim. In a nasty argument, Jonathan told Tim he'd only gotten into Brown because he was black. The fight touched off an intense debate among other students. White kids I knew who had always supported affirmative action in principle were suddenly critical of it in practice. Ultimately, the controversy made me work harder, made me even more competitive. For the first time, I felt that I had something to prove to my white peers, determined to make sure that if I was accepted at a prestigious college, nobody would be able to accuse me of being anything less than worthy.

By the end of tenth grade, I'd made up my mind that I would go to Harvard. Dad, of course, had made it abundantly clear that he expected me to attend a first-rate college; but the main reason I wanted to go to Harvard was my grandmother. Good hadn't had the chance to go to college, and she carried the hurt of that denial with her all her life. To my grandmother, an education represented the keys to the kingdom. Hadn't it been books, as much as anything, that the masters wanted to keep away from the slaves? Good believed that a college degree offered protection from the hardship of life; an education was something no white man could ever take away from you. The first person in our family to go to college had been my Aunt Thelma, my grandmother's younger sister. Good had helped pay

Thelma's way through Paine College in Augusta, Georgia. One winter the two of them shared a single coat—one sister being warm, the other shivering, on alternate days—so Thelma could have sufficient funds for school. In the next generation, my father attended Morehouse, "the Harvard of black colleges," as he called it. Now I felt it was my duty, my historic obligation, to go to the original. I didn't really know anything about Harvard—only that it was considered the best. I would go to Harvard, I told myself, because I owed it to my family to go. I would go to Harvard so that my own children could feel free to go to any college they damn well pleased.

My father decided it was time we moved. Our neighborhood had been coming apart for years. As white families left the area, services deteriorated. Fewer police patrolled the streets. Garbage piled up on the sidewalks. The landlord and superintendent grew lax about keeping the building clean and in working order. Muggings, burglaries, rapes, once rarities in our neighborhood, had become routine. Like the white families before us, we fled.

We moved to Riverdale, one of the last enclaves of affluence in the Bronx. The most exclusive part of Riverdale abounded with huge houses and meticulously manicured lawns. The more urban section was composed of drab, blocky apartment buildings with high rents and grandiose names like the Whitehall, the Century or Parkway House. My father, Bert and I lived in a three-bedroom apartment in one of the less grandiose buildings, the Greenwood, on a quiet, leafy street, about five blocks from Fieldston. We were the only black people in the largely Jewish building. The move was, in one sense, another slap to my mother. For years, she had pleaded with Dad to move us from our crumbling neighborhood; and for years, he had refused. Now that he had kicked Mom out of his home, he was prepared to transfer to a nicer one, leaving her behind. Soon after we moved, however, Mom took an apartment in the Kingsbridge section of the Bronx, just outside Riverdale, so she could be closer to us.

Living in Riverdale, I began, for the first time in my life and with no effort whatsoever, to terrify ordinary pedestrians. Walking down the street on a sunny morning, my bookbag slung over my shoulder, I'd see an elderly man or woman strolling ahead of me. As I drew within, say, five yards, the old person would sense my presence and turn around. The reaction was always the same. First, a flash of terror in the eyes. Then the stroller would stop dead in his tracks. Seemingly paralyzed with fear, he'd stare wide-eyed at me as I passed. The first several times this happened, I smiled as warmly as I could, trying to convey that I meant no harm. But it was no use. My smile was always returned by that wretched, panic-stricken stare, as if I were some leering sociopath. After a while I didn't bother acknowledging the frightened strollers. I was usually halfway down the block before they felt safe enough to resume their constitutionals. The aged suburbanites were even more alarmed by my friend Roy, who, by the eleventh grade, was already close to six and a half feet tall. "It makes me *want* to mug them," Roy used to say. "I mean, if that's what they assume I'm gonna do anyway, then why the hell not?"

But it was Roy who became a target. One Friday evening, Roy and Peter, a white classmate from Fieldston, were walking down First Avenue on the Upper East Side of Manhattan, a "good" neighborhood, when five or six white teenagers started following them. The kids were drinking beer and talking loud, playing heavy-metal noise on a boom box and coming up closer behind Roy and Peter. "Hey, nigger!" they called out. They mocked the "big nigger" and his friend, the "nigger lover." Roy and Peter kept on walking, pretending not to hear. This continued for several blocks until suddenly one of the kids slammed Roy over the head with the boom box. When Roy looked up again, dazed, he and Peter were surrounded. The leader of the gang waved a broken beer bottle. "Wanna fight, nigger?" Manhattanites passed by, briefly surveyed the scene, then walked on. "C'mon, nigger, let's fight." A white bouncer stared from the door of a nightclub just a few feet away. Roy and Peter moved toward the door. The bouncer blocked their path. "Keep it on the street," he said. "C'mon, nigger," the kid with the bottle taunted, "I'll cut your face open." One of the kids knocked Peter down. As he scrambled to get up from the sidewalk, another kid kicked him in the face. Roy, adrenaline churning in his fear and rage, shoved the kicker, knocking him flat on his ass. This freaked the gang out. The kid jumped to his feet and the whole bunch of them bolted up First Avenue.

As Roy told me of the incident, I felt that an outside world I'd known nothing of had come crashing in on our secure, ethically cultured lives. This was the sort of thing I'd thought only happened in the Deep South, redneck country. Or maybe in Boston. That such a thing could happen in New York City—in Manhattan, which I had always regarded as the epicenter of cultural enlightenment and tolerance—was nearly beyond my imagining. But the assault on Roy and Peter was only a prelude to the racial violence that would become ever more commonplace in New York. In early 1978 the reign of brutality was just beginning.

.   .   .

Though I had suspected for years that my father was habitually unfaithful to my mother, I'd never pictured Another Woman. Dad's infidelity was an abstraction to me, a parade of nameless, faceless bimbos. But early in my senior year of high school, Dad began making occasional references to a woman on the Upper West Side of Manhattan. He started talking openly on the phone with her when Bert and I were well within earshot. He was preparing us.

My father invited Bert and me to meet him downtown for dinner one autumn night. Arriving late at Dad's office building, we found him parked outside. A woman sat beside him in the darkened car, her face obscured by a cloud of cigarette smoke. Dad introduced us as Bert and I slid into the back seat. Her name was Ruth. I was not surprised to see that she was white. But Ruth's race hardly mattered to me. I was ready to dislike Dad's mistress regardless of her color.

We drove to a fancy seafood restaurant. Sitting across the table from Ruth, I went on conversational automatic pilot, prattling about my college applications and other banalities but not hearing my own words, too busy scrutinizing this interloper. Between the bits of small talk, I learned that Ruth, a tall, chunky woman with short brown hair and freckles on her cheeks and hands, was a middle-level executive in a large corporation. She was a widow, probably in her mid-forties, with a son in law school and a daughter at college. As a youngster, she'd spent several years in Jamaica, where her father had a business. She had a raspy, smoke-and-whiskey voice; her manner was, at once, gracious and no-nonsense—the tough dame with an air of sophistication. As the dinner progressed, I became aware of the rapport between Ruth and Dad. They finished each other's sentences, bantered good-naturedly, mirrored one another's gestures unselfconsciously. Ruth was completely unintimidated by my father, and my father clearly felt no need to try to intimidate Ruth. Pointing a finger at me, Dad turned to her and said, "This boy was walking, by himself on his own two feet, at nine months old! You believe that?"

Smiling slyly, Ruth said, "Well, with you kicking his ass, it's no wonder."

After dinner, we went to Ruth's labyrinthine, antique-filled apartment for coffee. She showed us a faded black-and-white photo taken when she was in her teens: Ruth stood on a beach in a white shirt and blue jeans, a Cheshire cat smile on her face; in one hand, she brandished a shot-gun; in the other, she held up a slimy alligator, its long tail trailing on the ground, that she had just bagged with a single shot. I had to laugh; my father, it seemed, had met his match.

Watching my father and Ruth chatting on the couch together, I couldn't help but feel that the affection between them was deep, genuine. But, at the same time, I sensed that Dad saw Ruth as some sort of prize, one more mark of his success, one more thing denied him in his youth that he had grown up to obtain. "Where I come from," Dad once said, "a nigger could get his dick chopped off just for *thinking* about screwin' a white woman." At the restaurant, I noticed how Dad clutched Ruth's hand and held it high as he guided her from the door to our table, almost as if he were flaunting her, his proud possession, defying the other diners—or his sons?—to say anything about it. Dad reveled in the casual opulence of Ruth's apartment. While she fixed coffee in the kitchen, he pointed to a painting on the wall and said to Bert and me, "That picture's worth two hundred thousand dollars. You believe that? Now that's what I call *art!*"

We would get together with Ruth several more times

that year and, despite my resistance, I grew to like her.
While my mother tried to obtain information from me, I did
everything I could to avoid talking about Ruth with her.
When Mom had learned that Dad was involved with a white
woman, she took it as the ultimate insult. Ruth would come
to signify the corruption of my mother's marriage, the outside agitator who disrupted her happy union, the thing
Mom had been looking for: a reason. I grew accustomed to
Mom referring to Ruth as "that white bitch."

My acceptance letter arrived at Christmastime. Good was at
our apartment that morning and she was the first person I
showed the note to. A long, slow, satisfied smile crept
across my grandmother's face. "Congratulations, sugar,"
she said. My father was a bit more demonstrative. I handed
him the letter as he got home from the office that evening.
Dad waved it in the air and whooped triumphantly. "We did
it!" he cried. "We got into Harvard! We got into Harvard!"
I said nothing, but I was extremely annoyed. What did he
mean *we*?

CHAPTER 6

MY FATHER'S HOME was a totalitarian state. Lying in my bed, staring into the darkness, unable to sleep, I found this idea so obvious, I could hardly believe it hadn't occurred to me before. Dad was the great dictator, demanding unthinking loyalty and obedience from his subjects. In the past, the most minor signs of rebellion or independence of thought were violently crushed. After the terror, Dad would play the benevolent fascist, making kindly gestures, rewarding our submission with money or presents. When Dad had had enough of a subject—his wife, say—that person was disappeared, then purged from history as if she never existed. Dad was his own minister of propaganda, telling you exactly what you were supposed to think of him. And I had been his silent collaborator, too frightened to speak up, cowed and cajoled into doing what was expected of me.

It was the summer of 1980 and I was back in Riverdale, back in my father's home after my freshman year at Harvard. I'd discovered that first year of college something I had not known was in me: an anger. I didn't really know where it came from; I didn't know what to do with it; but I carried it with me all the time.

I'd found Harvard to be a dull, cold, segregated place where, in the first several weeks of school, students scram-

bled to join the appropriate clique. Walking into the freshman dining hall for the first time and seeing, along one wall,
three tables filled exclusively with black students, I felt that
my social place had been preassigned. The young people at
the "black tables" were no different from other Harvard
students who found solace in sameness. There were Asian
tables, Wasp tables, Jewish tables, jock tables, gay tables,
nerd tables: every undergraduate tribe imaginable staked
out its turf in the Freshman Union.

Harvard made Fieldston look like a paradise of racial
and social harmony. Never had I felt my otherness to whites
so acutely. Some white students I met seemed shocked as
soon as I opened my mouth. To me, my voice sounded flat,
lacking in character. To them, it sounded bizarre. I'd been
talking to a white Midwesterner for about two minutes
when, staring in apparent astonishment, he asked, "Where
are you *from*?" A young white woman remarked, "You don't
sound like a black person." Who am I supposed to sound
like? I asked. Uncle Remus?

The national debate over affirmative action dragged on
interminably at Harvard, with some scholars implying that
blacks were inherently inferior students, below the stan-
dards of the great universities. I found this argument particularly fatuous when I made acquaintance with some of the
less illustrious Harvard students who had allegedly been
accepted on "merit." Students like the hockey player who
practically boasted about his low grades and SAT scores,
but whose athletic talent had won him admission. Or the
charming, wealthy young man whose performance in one of
my English classes indicated that he had nary a brain in his
finely chiseled head. He'd been rejected from every college
he'd applied to, except Harvard, the alma mater of his
father and grandfather. It seemed to me it would take at

least a couple more centuries before the number of mediocre black students admitted to Harvard even approached
the number of white mediocrities who had been accepted
at the school over the previous three hundred years.

But African Americans at Harvard were often made to
feel like unwanted guests who had been reluctantly invited
to the party, against the better judgment of the hosts. So I
could understand how many black students preferred to
keep to themselves, not wanting to take part in the larger
life of the university, not wanting to be judged by the stan-
dards of an institution that seemed, at best, iffy toward our
presence. Given what was happening at other colleges, one
sometimes felt almost under siege. During my first semester, I heard about a black woman at another Ivy League
university getting a bucket of urine poured on her as she
walked past a fraternity house. That was just the beginning:
nearly every month over the next four years, I would read
of some new racial incident on campuses across the country.

Yet, I rarely felt comfortable in circumscribed black
cliques. The protectiveness of grouping together could
prove stifling. To some students, having white friends made
me somehow suspect, as if I were fraternizing with the
enemy. They seemed to go through college always on
guard, expecting racism at every turn. I didn't want to live
my life that way.

By the end of my first semester, I felt as if I were in a
social limbo. I avoided getting linked to any clique, but
every time I passed the black tables without taking a seat,
I felt a twinge of guilt, as if I were breaking some rule,
betraying some obligation. Ultimately, I wound up being
more guarded than anyone. Though I always had friends,
I didn't allow many people at Harvard to get close to me.

The breezy cordiality I displayed with most everyone masked the growing anger I felt. I was angry at all the people, white and black, whom I saw as small-minded, bigoted and shallow. And I was angry at myself, for while all I wanted was to be accepted as myself, I feared that the self I cherished so much was terminally ambivalent.

If there was one trait that most Harvard students shared, it was an obsessive careerism. As early as freshman week, one encountered students planning for law school, medical school, business school. The artistically inclined were, if anything, even more single-minded and purposeful than the preprofessional set. I was no different. I had known for a long time that I wanted to be a writer. Writing was what I'd always done best and loved most; teachers at Fieldston had always been enthusiastic and encouraging about my work. Writing would dominate my life at Harvard. I joined the student daily newspaper, the *Crimson,* as a film and theater critic, hoping to learn how to write precisely and entertainingly on deadline. I enrolled in fiction-writing workshops and churned out short stories compulsively. I experimented with essay assignments, writing a paper on *The Wild Palms,* for instance, in Faulknerian prose. I even approached love letters as opportunities to hone my style. I didn't know what sort of writing I ultimately wanted to do. I didn't know how I could make a living writing after college. But I knew that I wanted to give it a shot. Only one person stood between me and my goal.

I called Dad in November of my freshman year to tell him I was trying out for a position on the *Crimson.*

"Business staff, of course," Dad said.

"No, editorial."

"What do you want to do that for?"

"I want to write."

"Aw, c'mon, man, that's not gonna get you anywhere."

I tried a different approach. "The *Crimson*'s a good paper, Dad. It's a great credential for anything I might want to do after college."

"Well, maybe you could write on business. I'll get you a subscription to *Barron's.*"

"I just don't think business writing is my forte, Dad."

"I don't care what your *forte* is. I didn't send you to Harvard to waste your time on meaningless shit. I sent you there to get marketable skills."

Going to Harvard was just one step in my father's master plan for me. "My son is going to be the best damned lawyer in New York," Dad liked to say. Though I'd never said I wanted to go to law school, by refraining to say that I did not want to go, I'd only acquiesced to my father's fantasies. Tossing and turning in my narrow bed in Grays Hall, I struggled to find some way to please my father and myself: *So maybe I'll go to law school, it might not be so bad. Then; then maybe I can be my own person, do what I want to do. Of course, I'll have to practice law for a few years, but that's okay. Maybe I'll just be a lawyer for five or six years. Then; maybe then . . .*

I spent weeks trying to convince my father that American History and Literature was a worthwhile major. He finally agreed when he learned how many History and Lit. graduates went on to law school. I wanted to spend the summer after my freshman year waiting tables with a friend on Long Island. Dad was repulsed by the idea of *his son* doing such menial labor. If I spent the summer working in a restaurant, my father said, he would not "subsidize" me during my sophomore year. He knew how to get me. I did what Dad wanted, returning to New York that summer to take a clerical job.

My friend Roy was also back in New York that summer, after his freshman year at Brown, counseling kids at a foster care institution in Westchester and living with his parents in Riverdale. He had experienced the same conundrum in Providence that I had in Cambridge, feeling pressured to socialize more with black students and to shun whites. "It's like being a Martian," Roy used to say of not fitting other people's expectations of how a black student was supposed to act. Roy was a musician and his best friends at Brown, most of them white, were also musicians. The songs Roy wrote straddled musical categories. He composed in the pop, new wave, funk and R & B modes, finding his own voice in the amalgam of genres. That summer, we'd hang out together at his parents' place until the wee hours, collaborating on songs. I turned out to be a hamhanded lyricist, producing convoluted, virtually unsingable, doggerel. But we had fun. Let other people seek their identities in big, protective groups, I thought, let them have their cliques and fraternities; Roy and I were happiest in our circle of two.

By the time I'd return from Roy's place, my father, if he wasn't spending the night at Ruth's, would be fast asleep. In the morning Dad would give me a ride to work in Manhattan. Driving down the West Side Highway, Dad talked nonstop about his latest business venture. He was going through complex machinations to purchase a concrete manufacturing plant in New Jersey. He talked of the skyscrapers and freeways he was going to construct, of the bushels of money he would make. He planned to build an industry giant; someday, after I'd had some experience as a corporate lawyer, I would come work for him; then, once he retired, I would inherit his empire. As my father went on with his swirl of epic scenarios—*Million dollar deals . . . High-class partners . . . You'll take over someday*—he began to sound almost delusional to me. I sensed that Dad was headed for a terrible fall.

Most mornings, Dad would stop at Ruth's apartment building. I'd move from the front seat to the back so Ruth could sit beside my father. Driving into midtown, Dad and Ruth would regale me with anecdotes of the life they'd shared. Of the time when Dad taught Ruth's son how to drive. Of Dad's close relationship with Ruth's mother. Of the time they picked up Ruth's daughter from summer camp and the little girl had found a stray cat that she wanted to leave in the forest so it could live in its "natural habitat" and how hard Dad and Ruth laughed at that, and how they brought the cat home to Manhattan and how that cat loved to curl itself around my father's neck while he sat in his favorite armchair in Ruth's apartment. I never let on how painful it was for me to hear these stories; I just let them go on talking. I had a bitter desire to find out what my father had been doing when he hadn't had time for his wife and children. Dad and Ruth, I learned as I sat in the back seat, had carried on their affair for at least nine years. It was Ruth, a stranger to me until I was seventeen, who had suggested Fieldston as a good choice for my education, thus engineering one of the most significant changes in my life. I was stunned to hear this. Gratitude clashed with a sense of exposure, of intimacy violated. What other decisions in the life of my family, I wondered, had Ruth helped set into motion?

Dad always dropped Ruth off about a block away and

around the corner from the entrance to her office building. After she got out of the car one morning, my father explained why. He didn't dare take her right to the door for fear that one of her colleagues might see her with a black man. My presence in the back seat, presumably, must have doubled their apprehension: imagine Ruth's embarrassment at being seen in a car with *two* black men. Perhaps Dad was content to be regarded as an object of shame, I thought, but I was sickened by the little subterfuge and wanted no part of it. I started taking the bus or the subway into Manhattan every morning.

My father and I waged a war of little digs that summer, addressing each other in impatient, patronizing tones, taunting each other with exasperated sighs and muttered sarcasm. But mainly, we didn't speak at all. Some mornings, I'd hear Dad screaming at colleagues on the phone. "Just get it done!" . . . "What the fuck are you wasting my time for!" . . . "Your incompetence is gonna cost us this whole fucking deal!" This was something new. I was accustomed to my father's verbal assaults on the people who loved him, but I'd never heard him lash out at business associates. I gleaned from Dad's vehement end of the conversations that the deal for the concrete plant was in jeopardy. But I didn't ask my father what was going on, and he didn't offer any information. "Don't tell me it can't be done! I want the papers on my desk tomorrow or it's gonna be your ass!" The tirades invariably ended with Dad slamming down the receiver.

Ruth invited me to join her and Dad for dinner one night in August. At the restaurant, she asked about my work for the *Crimson.*

"Don't encourage him," Dad said. I rolled my eyes in irritation. "I don't know why you waste your time on that crap," he continued. "I'm not sending you to Harvard to fuck around. I'm sending you there to get—"

"Marketable skills. Yeah, I know."

"Damn straight."

Ignoring my father, I engaged Ruth in a discussion of books, plays, films and music that Dad knew little about. Ruth and I went on for a good half hour, the talk getting more animated, while my father sat in glum silence, squirming and looking around the restaurant, ordering another drink, drumming the table impatiently with his fingers. When the conversation turned to philosophy, Dad jumped in. "You can't even talk about philosophy if you haven't read Descartes. Have you read Descartes?"

"No," I said.

"I've read Descartes. The complete works, cover to cover. I think, therefore I am. I know all a that shit. I can even tell you how Cartesian theory influenced Socrates."

"Sorry, Dad," I said, with a lavish smirk, "but I can't imagine Descartes had too much of an influence on Socrates when Socrates lived about two thousand years before him."

My father looked startled. I could see, behind his eyes, that he knew he'd made a mistake; but he was not about to concede the point. "You're wrong. Descartes came before Socrates."

"That's just not correct, Dad."

"I'm telling you it's right. Descartes came before Socrates."

"That's impossible, Dad. You're wrong."

"Don't tell me I'm wrong!" Other diners turned and looked at our table.

"But you are."

"You're full of shit! Descartes came centuries before Socrates!"

"You must know that's not true!"

"Don't tell me it's not true!"

If you have ever witnessed an act of sudden violence—whether it was in a barroom, on a city street, or in your parents' home—you might know of that moment just before the first strike occurs, when time freezes and violence becomes inevitable. My father and I, sitting across from each other in a crowded restaurant, had arrived at that moment and just as we got there, Ruth blurted out, "Let's order dessert!" The argument was over. My father and I did not speak to each other for the rest of the meal. But that moment of previolence, that vacuum of tension, would be stretched out over the next two weeks. We would live in that moment, brushing silently past each other in the apartment, expectant and wary.

A week before I was due back at Harvard for the start of my sophomore year, I received a letter from the financial aid office. My father, it said, was months late on my tuition payments and had failed to sign and return important forms on my loan and grant status. Unless the matter was resolved, I would not be allowed to register for the new semester. That night I left a petulant note on my father's pillow, telling him to get this problem straightened out. I went to bed before Dad got home.

My father paces wildly around his bedroom, waving my note in the air. "Where the fuck do you get off telling me what to do! How dare you tell me what to do!" It's eight o'clock in the morning and he has not yet finished dressing for work. I notice how large his stomach has grown, stretching the material of his white undershirt. I stand in the center of his bedroom, my arms folded across my chest, saying nothing.

"You think I'm made of money! You think I can just come up with money whenever *you* need it! Who the fuck do you think you are? One of your rich white friends?"

You can't let this get to you. You can't let this get to you . . .

"What the hell is your problem, man? What kind of shit are you trying to pull? You wanna hate me 'cause of what happened with your mother? You wanna hate me for that!"

But I haven't even mentioned Mom. What's he talking about?

"Children can't hate their parents! I'm not gonna have it! Maybe you saw me go a little crazy that night. Okay, fine. But we're not gonna have this fucked-up father-son bull-shit! I don't have time for this crap! I won't allow it!"

I glare at my father, biting the insides of my cheeks, saying nothing.

"You think you're smarter than me?" Dad is standing not six inches in front of me now, his mouth twisted in rage. "You think you're smarter than me? Do you! You can't find your way to the bathroom without me!"

We stare hard into each other's eyes.

"You think you're better than me? Huh? You think you're better than me!"

I feel that in the next second my father is going to strike me. And then it happens: the sudden realization, a dead certainty I feel, and see mirrored back in my father's eyes as doubt. No, I do not hate my father. I do not think I'm smarter than him, or better; but I am, at nineteen, taller, leaner, and twenty-nine years younger than my father, and if he lays a finger on me, I will jump all over him. And looking into my father's eyes, I can see that he doesn't like his odds.

Finally, Dad turns away. "Get outta my sight." I leave

his room, drained, exhausted, but perfectly calm. The lines have been redrawn.

Back at Harvard, over the next three years, I felt as if my real life had not yet begun; that it couldn't begin until I graduated from college and stopped needing my father. I scored high grades in the courses I liked and mediocre ones in the classes that bored me. I spent long afternoons watching double features at the gloriously decrepit Harvard Square Cinema. I performed in a few plays, made some invaluable friends, and succumbed to a stream of feverish infatuations; and I wrote.

Dad got his concrete plant, but his financial problems only worsened. Checks from home frequently bounced. I became a regular guest at the financial aid office, apologizing for our tardiness in making tuition payments and filling out forms. Dad and I communicated only through terse, businesslike notes and phone calls. When I visited New York, I stayed with friends, avoiding my father's home. My mother's illnesses grew more severe and debilitating. I rarely spoke with my brother or sister. I didn't see my grandmother much, but Good still sent me Federal Express packages of fried chicken during exam periods.

In the fall of my senior year, Dad's business went under again. He called me to explain how certain deals he'd been relying on had fallen through. "What are you telling me, Dad?" I snapped, nearly hysterical. "That we have no money? Is that what you're telling me?" Dad insisted that he would bounce back from this financial crisis just as he had bounced back in the past. I didn't believe him.

While my father's financial collapse was, in one sense, a nightmare come true, it was also a sort of liberation.

Money was the last tangible form of power my father held over me, the threat of a financial cutoff the last lever he could pull to get me to do what he wanted. Now that power was gone; and with it, any notion I'd ever entertained about going to law school. I could finally pursue a writing career without opposition.

In June 1983, Harvard, grudgingly but mercifully, allowed me to graduate even though we still owed months of tuition. The week of my commencement I had an overdrawn bank account and $25,000 worth of debts. My father called three days before I graduated to say he would be too busy to attend the ceremony. "I don't care," I said. It would be more than five years before my father and I would speak to each other again.

PART 2

EVERY WORKDAY MORNING, I donned my disguise: the shirt with the button-down collar, the skinny tie, the baggy pants, the jacket (tweed in fall and winter, dark blue blazer in spring and summer) and the black shoes which, in a small private act of defiance, I rarely shined, deliberately letting them get scuffed and dusty. And so, protected by my corporate camouflage, I made my way through the better part of the eighties, waiting out a hard-hearted decade, trying to construct as tranquil a life for myself as possible. I wasn't looking to beat the system; I didn't want to join the system. I just wanted to manipulate it.

My mother was laughing, an open, full-throated, giddy laugh; her better laugh. We sat in a coffee shop near Rockefeller Center, remembering some silly incident from a long time ago. My mother's office was directly across the street from mine and every couple of weeks we had lunch together. And though we'd been doing this for more than five years now, every lunch felt like a long-delayed reunion. As we rose to head back to work, Mom asked, "So, have you heard anything from your daddy yet?"

She asked the question mainly out of habit since my

answer was always the same. But on this day, I actually had some news. "As a matter of fact," I told Mom, "some detective called looking for Dad the other morning."

My mother looked startled. After I recounted my brief conversation with the private investigator, Mom asked if I was going to call my father. "I don't know," I said, and abruptly changed the subject. I didn't tell Mom that the night before I had rummaged through my file cabinet and located the slip of paper Bert had given me with Dad's number scribbled on it. Still, I couldn't bring myself to pick up the phone. Calling my father, I felt, would be like talking to a ghost.

Five and a half years earlier, the day after my college graduation, I'd moved into an apartment in Greenwich Village with two friends from Harvard. I phoned Dad at his office but he never returned my calls. The office soon shut down. I called him in Riverdale but there was never any answer. The telephone company eventually cut off his service. I sent Dad notes telling him where I was living and that I'd like to see him. No response. I tried contacting him through Ruth, but he had withdrawn from her as well. Bert, forced by Dad's financial implosion to drop out of the University of Pennsylvania after his freshman year, moved in with my mother and took a job as an office clerk at a law firm. Under threat of eviction, Dad left the Riverdale apartment, telling my grandmother he was moving to Yonkers. He didn't give her a forwarding address. "Your daddy was so obsessed with money and success," Mom said at the time, "now that he doesn't have it, I guess he just can't face anybody." After not hearing from Dad for a year, I decided to shut him out of my mind. As far as I was concerned, my father was dead.

Felicia fell in love and married a man of uncommon

kindness and decency. We celebrated most birthdays and holidays at my sister's home in northern Westchester. After dinner, Lish and Bert and I would go off to the study and talk, mainly just filling each other in on what was going on in our lives. There was an odd sort of camaraderie when we talked about the family and the past, remembering old battles as if we were war veterans who'd once shared the same foxhole. When, after two years out of school, Bert reenrolled at Penn, the rest of us pitched in to help him with tuition payments and other financial necessities. In Dad's absence, I came to fill a special role in the family, dispensing advice and support, smoothing over misunderstandings among the others.

My mother linked arms with me as we left the coffee shop and walked down 50th Street. As she spoke animatedly about some controversy at the office, I thought how good it felt just to have an ordinary conversation with her. When I was younger, my mother's fragility had made me want to keep some distance between us. But my detachment had only exacerbated her troubles. Since leaving college, I'd felt a need for absolution. I didn't consider myself a religious person. Torn between my mother's devotion and my father's atheism, I'd wound up thoroughly agnostic; believing in God made no more or less sense to me than not believing. But Catholicism had left its mark on me. I felt that by having been less than totally committed to my mother, I had sinned. I wanted to make up for that. After trying so hard to be the perfect son to my father, I now tried to be the man my mother wanted me to be. I wanted to help her get over all the bad things that had happened to her. I wanted to redeem my mother's life.

"Don't you have any gloves?" Mom asked suddenly.

"They're in my pockets."

"Well, put them on your hands," she ordered, "it's cold out."

"Okay."

"And don't forget to send your Aunt Lucille a card, it's—"

"I know, I remember."

"And I told you, Felicia wants you to bring a bottle of champagne to her house for Thanksgiving."

"Right."

We arrived at the entrance of Mom's office building. "So," she said, "you'll call me this Sunday?"

"Of course."

"Button up your coat."

"I only have to walk across the street, Mom."

"Button it up, anyway. It's cold out here."

"All right."

She kissed me goodbye. "Talk to you Sunday. I love you."

"Love you too."

By the time I interviewed with Player—two months before my college graduation—I was pretty sure I had the job locked up. Player was the quintessential company man. Tall, lanky, graying at the temples, he welcomed me into his office with a bonhomie that was no less disarming for being clearly well-rehearsed. Along the wall an array of trophies glittered, prizes garnered during his years as captain of the *Time* softball team. I asked Player about the magazine's reputation for ultraconservative politics. *Time*'s right-wing bias, he said, had died with its founder, Henry Luce. The magazine's political slant, if it had one at all, was firmly middle of the road and had been so for the past fifteen years. From what I'd read in *Time*, I couldn't agree with Player entirely, but, I figured, what the hell, I wasn't going to be writing on politics anyway. I was hoping for a job writing on the arts and popular culture.

Then came the line I'd been anticipating. "I won't beat around the bush," Player said amiably. "Your chances of getting a job here are enhanced by your being black."

I had a response ready. "I know my race will be taken into account," I said earnestly, "but I hope that the main factor will be the quality of my writing."

Player beamed. "I assure you it will."

My final interview was with a somber, portly editor who sat behind an immaculate desk in an office so dimly lit that I could only make out my interrogator in silhouette. "Do you prefer to be called Jacob or Jake?" he asked from the shadows.

"Jake," I replied.

"Very well. I shall call you Mr. Lamar."

He went on to tell me how grateful I should feel just to be considered for this job. Leaving the editor's office, I was stopped by his secretary, a prim woman with the countenance of a Mother Superior. "Jacob," she said gravely, "we *want* you to do well here."

I started work at *Time* ten days after leaving Cambridge. On a New York staff of about sixty writers, I was one of two African Americans. People told me there had been a "revolving door" of black writers who had lasted less than a year in the job. Some, I was informed, had had trouble mastering Timestyle, the magazine's peculiar mode of prose. This didn't worry me. At twenty-two, I knew I wasn't as good a writer as I could be. I knew I'd probably never be as good as I wanted to be. But I'd read enough of the magazine to know that I was good enough to write for *Time*.

Other black writers, I was told, had failed to "fit in" to
Time's Waspy, Ivy League atmosphere. The last black
writer, it was whispered, had been a little "paranoid," a bit
"oversensitive." This did worry me—but not very much.
Having spent a few summers working in offices, I figured I
knew how to negotiate the social Kabuki of corporate race
relations.

During my first week on the job, a jocular man with
bushy eyebrows and a thick Southern accent introduced
himself to me as the affirmative action recruiter for the
writing staff. "Where did you come from?" he asked, looking bewildered.

"College," I said. "I just graduated a couple of weeks
ago."

"From where?"

"Harvard."

"Hmm. And how did you wind up at *Time*?"

"A professor of mine introduced me to a senior writer
here and he passed my clips on to the editors."

"Ah, the old-boy network."

"I guess."

"Well, how is it I never heard of you? I recruited at
Harvard."

I told him I'd been on the staff of the *Crimson* for four
years. Did he recruit there?

"Why, no," he said as if the thought had never occurred to him.

If he hadn't looked for black journalists at Harvard's
daily student newspaper, where had he looked? The weekly
newspaper, the *Independent*?

"Why, no," he said.

The *Advocate,* the campus's main literary magazine?
"No."

The *Lampoon*?

"No."

He had simply asked for the names of a few students from teachers in the expository writing department. Expository writing, a course required for all freshmen, taught the most basic elements of essay construction. I was too surprised to ask him why he hadn't recruited at the major student publications. Perhaps he'd assumed that since there were practically no black writers at *Time*, there wouldn't be too many at Harvard either.

Deborah was a coltish, quick-witted young woman I knew at Harvard, one of the few people I'd felt genuinely close to there. Shortly after I graduated, when I'd first started writing for *Time* and Deborah was working in New York for the summer, we fell in love. I knew Deborah's family fairly well. She once told me that her father, a successful lawyer, had been particularly fond of me. That was before I started going out with his daughter. When he learned of our relationship, he was angrier than Deborah had ever seen him. Her mother took a more pragmatic tack: "Just don't marry him," she said. I was shocked. Here were people who'd enjoyed my company in their home, who considered themselves open-minded liberals—yet, they'd turned against me overnight. And though Deborah and I had been dating for only two or three weeks and had not thought even fleetingly about marriage, it was the prospect of matrimony and children that her parents threw up as the ultimate nightmare. This was the closet bigot's last stand: Yes, you can move into my neighborhood, you can attend my schools, you can run my local government; but you cannot touch my children, you cannot mix your blood with mine—this is where integration ends.

Deborah, though upset by her parents' reaction, denied they were racists. Like a lot of well-intentioned white people, Deborah found it inconceivable that any average white person she knew could be a racist. The civil rights movement had revealed the horror of racism so effectively that few whites could see it as something ordinary. They seemed to regard it as somehow passé, something that had disappeared from American life after the sixties. Racists were people like George Wallace or grand wizards of the Ku Klux Klan—not one of their friends, not Mom and Dad.

Despite her parents' disapproval, Deborah and I continued seeing each other that summer. Though the romance soured after she returned to Harvard in the fall, our friendship endured. But whenever I thought about what had happened, I became angry all over again—and disgusted with myself. Disgusted by my naivete, my grandiosity. Because I had thought I was immune. I thought that any white person who actually knew me couldn't possibly hold my race against me. Hadn't I gone to Harvard? Wasn't I the two things that magazines like *Time* always cited when judging a black person acceptable: "articulate" and "nonthreatening"? I realized there was a ferocious black tax in this country; but I'd allowed myself to believe that my education, my sociability, my bourgeois credentials, made me exempt. Deborah's parents taught me that every black person, sooner or later, one way or another, had to pay.

My first six months at *Time* were spent writing Milestones, a weekly tally of the deaths and childbirths, marriages and divorces, indictments and convictions of the famous and infamous. Milestone items were extremely short, perhaps a hundred and fifty words at the longest. I approached Milestones as a sort of word game, trying to pack as much information and bright language as possible into such a tight space, and I often enjoyed the column immensely.

But occasionally, I was called on to perform a less pleasant task. Every issue of *Time* opened with the Letter from the Publisher, in which readers were told of some courageous correspondent tracking down a big story in a dangerous corner of the globe, or of the tireless and dedicated, skyscraper-bound staff in the New York office who orchestrated the magazine's mighty resources to produce this week's cover story. It was exceedingly difficult to be quoted in the "Publetter" without sounding like a twit, though most staffers who were profiled seemed to enjoy seeing themselves in the photos that accompanied each column. The tone of the Publetter was that of a proud father marveling at the accomplishments of his gifted children. Yet, the publisher of *Time* never wrote the Publetter. The column, essentially a public relations release, was ghostwritten every week, ordinarily by a low-level staff writer. And while I cranked out a number of Publetters, I never once laid eyes on the man whose signature appeared below the columns I had written.

Except for soliciting quotations for the Publetter and a month spent in the Washington bureau, I did little reporting for *Time*. The magazine neatly divided responsibility for the form and content of most of its articles. Correspondents based in bureaus around the world supplied the bulk of the content, basically emptying their notebooks into computers and relaying the jumble of details, quotes and on-the-scene color to the Time-Life Building in Rockefeller Center. There, writers received the correspondents' "files," combined them with information gathered by the New York research staff, and shaped the material into stories. This was fine by me. I'd never enjoyed reporting. On the *Crimson,* I'd written film and theater reviews, never breaking news stories. At best, a *Time* writer could bring to life a mass of disparate elements, crafting a story to fit his or her own perspective on the news, putting a distinctive personal stamp on a piece. At worst, we were simply doing a journalistic shoeshine, buffing and polishing other people's work.

There were three levels of writer on the *Time* masthead, with staff writers at the bottom of the order. Associate editors were essentially staff writers who had written three or more cover stories. Associate editors generally had a choice of two career paths at *Time.* One was to become a senior writer: these were the virtuosos of Timestyle, well-paid wordsmiths who had their pick of the best stories. The other option was to become a senior editor.

Senior editors formulated and assigned stories, tinkered with them once they were written, selected photos to illustrate the articles, made sure that deadlines were met, and went to endless meetings. There were twelve senior editors when I joined *Time* in 1983: eleven were white men, one was a white woman, most had attended either Harvard, Yale or Princeton. Though senior editors shouldered a large degree of responsibility and made fine salaries, they occupied a precarious position in the corporate pyramid of fear.

Lifer was representative of the breed. He was a dapper, middle-aged senior editor who worked mainly in the "back of the book"—sections that included Milestones, Science, Religion, Books, Cinema, Music, etc.—but who sometimes did stints in the "front of the book": World, Economy and Business, and *Time*'s most prominent, high-pressured section, Nation. A bit of a dilettante and a good talker, Lifer enjoyed leaning back in his chair and chatting up writers about sports and politics. But his geniality disappeared when the subject of the Managing Editor arose. "When the Managing Editor gets anxious," Lifer once said, his voice slightly aquiver, "he doesn't bite his fingernails. He bites *our* fingernails."

With his narrow eyes, iron-gray beard and Southern twang, the man who held the Managing Editor's office when I first arrived at *Time* had the aura of a Confederate general. Severely competitive, he was obsessed with outdoing *Time*'s rival newsmagazine, traditionally referred to in the office as "Brand X." The Managing Editor kept his distance from writers. We mainly heard from him in memos lecturing us on Timestyle. In a typical missive, circulated to the entire editorial staff, the M.E. railed against the use of colons and semicolons in the magazine. "They are for the most part abominations," the M.E. wrote sternly. "God created the period and the comma. Man made the rest." The M.E. was surrounded by a small cadre of enforcers known as "top editors"—two executive editors and three assistant managing editors. Lifer was nearly beside himself one morning when, after failing to make tiny changes in a story requested by an assistant managing editor, he received a furious phone call. "You ignore the top editor's comments," the top editor warned through clenched teeth, *"at your peril."* Once the General left the M.E.'s post and was succeeded by the more approachable Player, I thought the senior editors might relax. But their fear remained just as intense. They did not care who the M.E. was—just that he was the M.E.

But even the Managing Editor himself lived in fear of the figure at the very top of the food chain. As Editor-in-Chief, the Baron wielded ultimate control over all of Time Incorporated's seven major magazines from his office on the thirty-fourth floor, the building's corporate inner sanc-

....

tum. My only contact with the Baron came at lunches he arranged for writers and editors in one of the corporate dining rooms. A short, obese man with heavy-lidded eyes, a dense Bavarian accent and a taste for long, thin, brown cigarettes, he clearly relished lording over these affairs. At one of the first lunches I attended, the Baron ordered lobster tails, then fixed the waitress with a basilisk stare. "These *are* South African lobster tails?" he inquired. "Yessir," the waitress replied. The Baron nodded his approval. He spent the lunch making sweeping pronouncements on the state of national and international affairs, urging the editors and writers present to offer their thoughts. If someone put forth an opinion that swayed from his thinking—by questioning, for instance, U.S. involvement in Central America—the Baron, in crisp, sophistic tones, told them why their point of view was wrong and his was correct. Next topic. The lunch proceeded in this way, the Baron encouraging his subordinates to challenge his ideas, then swatting them down after they timidly took the bait. Seeing no gain in opening my mouth, I kept it shut.

Minuteman loved nuclear weapons. He reveled in scenarios of mutually assured destruction. He spoke ardently of ICBMs and INFs, of Midgetmen and MX missiles. So when the dean of one of America's nuclear war think tanks died, Minuteman volunteered to write his obituary. I was surprised that the star writer of the Nation section, renowned for relentlessly churning out one cover story after another, would want to muscle in on Milestones, but I was content to have him write the item. I first met Minuteman when I dropped by the Milestones editor's office to turn over the background material on the deceased doomsayer. Standing

no more than five and a half feet tall, with dirty-blond hair
clipped as neatly as a cadet's, Minuteman looked far
younger than his thirty-one years. Only his eyes gave him
away. They were enormous dark brown eyes, full of panic
and suspicion. Minuteman gave me a quick look up and
down as the Milestones editor introduced us. He gave my
hand a single, perfunctory shake. "Where you from?" he
asked, sounding vastly uninterested. "Chicago bureau? Detroit?"

"No," I said, feeling my back stiffen, "I've never even
been to Chicago or Detroit."

"Well, where did you work before?"

"Actually, I just graduated from college in June."

"Yeah, where'd you go?"

"Harvard."

Minuteman's face split into a gigantic grin. He grasped
my hand and shook it again, this time with discomforting
vigor. "No shit," he exclaimed. "I'm a Harvard man myself.
Pleased to meet you. What did you say your name was?"

Though he was only an associate editor in his sixth year
at *Time,* Minuteman was already legendary. To some, he
was a wunderkind, famous for his exhaustive knowledge of
American politics, his boundless appetite for work, and his
uncanny "news judgment"—the ability to predict with ac-
curacy what next month's big story would be. To others, he
was an impudent conniver who enjoyed harassing researchers and secretaries to the point of tears while passionately
toadying to his superiors. While some staffers thought Minuteman was destined to become Managing Editor someday,
others argued that the unseemly nakedness of his ambition
would do him in. "The lean and hungry look just doesn't
cut it around here," Lifer said. "Mark my words: that fellow
has gone as far as he's going to go in this organization."

Two weeks later, Minuteman was named deputy senior editor of the Nation section. I received a call from a top editor one morning informing me that I was about to be transferred from Milestones to Nation. "They're probably going to park you there for a while," he said. Minuteman, I learned, had asked specifically for me. I had little desire to write on national affairs but I knew that most staff writers, sooner or later, had to do a stint in the front of the book. Though I was the only black writer in the section, I did have something in common with many Nation staffers. Of the two editors and eight writers in the section, five of us had gone to Harvard. Minuteman loved the idea of having a little Cambridge Mafia in the Nation corridor.

As the section's most junior writer, I usually didn't deal with the hard-core political stories on the defense budget or foreign policy. I was put on the crime and punishment beat: drug busts, serial killings, trials and municipal scandals, stories with some measure of inherent drama. It was a painless job. I had a facility for Timestyle. I liked the pay. I got along well with the other writers, the researchers and secretaries in the section who, like the great majority of my *Time* colleagues, were bright, good-humored people. I didn't mind Nation's hours, though we generally worked until midnight on Thursdays, even later on Friday nights and often had to come into the office on Saturdays to make final changes on articles or write late-breaking stories hours before the magazine went to press. I had a certain detachment from the articles I wrote; the writing that was most important to me I did at home, in my notebooks, after office hours.

I'd hoped to make it through my stint in Nation without ever having to write about Ronald Reagan. Growing up, I regarded the right-wing California governor as a malevolent clown. I never imagined that a man of such profound ignorance, a man who bore such bald contempt for the poor and disenfranchised, a B-movie actor who spouted cornball slogans and cryptoracist rhetoric, could ever become president of the United States. Even my father the conservative couldn't stomach Reagan: Dad quit the Republican Party and became an Independent—which was my registration as well—when Reagan won the GOP nomination. After watching Reagan's victory speech at the *Crimson* office on election night 1980, I went back to my dorm and cried.

Now, more than three years later, the general public had become deeply infatuated with its TV star–president. *Time* eagerly joined in the Reagan lovefest. The magazine extolled him for leading America into a new "Era of Good Feelings." Editors liked referring to the President as "the Gipper" in the magazine. Though Reagan was completely dependent on his handlers and needed note cards to make his way through an ordinary meeting with congressmen, *Time* praised him as a wily chess player when it came to political strategy. When Reagan made comments like "There you go again" or "You ain't seen nothin' yet," *Time* hailed him for his rapier wit. Though transcripts of his press conferences and interviews proved that Reagan could barely articulate a spontaneous, coherent thought, *Time* saluted him as "the Great Communicator."

While pundits talked about Reagan's irresistible charisma or the appeal of his every-man-for-himself political message, I always thought that much of his White House popularity grew from having survived an assassination attempt barely two months into his presidency. It was a twisted, virtually subliminal sort of national redemption, as if JFK had risen from the back of the convertible with a shrug and a smile—"Hey, no problem, it was only a flesh wound." The only heroes America loved as much as its dead heroes were those who had cheated death.

Minuteman prided himself on being able to talk anybody's talk. If he was talking to me, he was an enthusiastic supporter of Jesse Jackson's presidential candidacy; when talking to a conservative top editor, he criticized Jackson as a loose cannon and a spoiler. He might passionately attack American support for the Nicaraguan contras at a meeting of writers in the morning, then, with a similar tone of conviction, argue in its favor at a lunch with the Baron that afternoon. When it came to covering the news, Minuteman had only one concern: what was the "hot" issue? He had a nose for trends, catchphrases and all things considered new. "We only have to be right for one week," Minuteman liked to say. This he considered objective journalism. And, for *Time* magazine, it was. Because while the top editors made sure that a conservative slant went on most of Nation's political stories, Minuteman generally liked the articles he edited to have an on-the-one-hand-on-the-other-hand structure that at least implied impartiality.

While I was moving into the camp that believed Minuteman would inevitably become Managing Editor, I saw one major obstacle in his path: the tall, bespectacled, meticulously well-mannered figure of Whiteshirt. Though only three or four years older than Minuteman, Whiteshirt was, as chief Nation editor, his immediate boss. Famous for his deft hand with copy, his diplomatic expertise in dealing with his colleagues, and his unflappability under pressure, Whiteshirt was smooth where Minuteman was coarse, his motives veiled while Minuteman's were transparent. His attire was the epitome of funereal professionalism. He favored dark suits with a sliver of white handkerchief poking from the breast pocket. And nearly every day of the week, he wore a crisp and immaculate snowy shirt with a button-down collar.

Though known for his friendliness, Whiteshirt barely acknowledged me during my first several months in Nation. I might receive, at most, a faint nod if we passed in the corridor. "He's just insecure 'cause he didn't get into Harvard," Minuteman said. "He only went to Penn." This hardly seemed like a reason to snub me; and, besides, half the writers in the section had gone to Harvard and Whiteshirt was quite chummy with the others.

The two Nation editors held a lunch for the section's writers at an elegant French restaurant. The conversation turned to football. After a while, someone noted the absence of Nation's only female writer, who was out sick that day. "What a vintage *Time* magazine luncheon," Whiteshirt said, with a smile and a touch of wistfulness in his voice. "A bunch of whi—"

He stopped short, glanced at me, quickly turned away, made a sound that was something between a laugh and a cough, and started his sentence again. "A bunch of men talking about sports."

Whiteshirt seemed to find it impossible to look me in the eye. I sometimes found myself in his office with Minuteman discussing a story. When I asked Whiteshirt a question, he would unfailingly turn to his deputy and answer it. On the unusual occasions when I talked with Whiteshirt alone, his frosty gaze seemed focused on a point on the wall behind me.

While Minuteman, Player and all the top editors had complimented my work, Whiteshirt was unimpressed. Reviewing one of the few foreign policy stories I'd written at that point, he criticized my saying that Reagan and one of his European counterparts had had a "constructive dia- logue." I had to admit it was a rather flat phrase. But for Whiteshirt, it had a most unsavory connotation. "Construc- tive dialogues," he said contemptuously, "are what *Third World* diplomats at the U.N. have." Critiquing another story of mine, he said, "You seem to have a good understanding of the English language."

Well, I thought to say, English *is* my first language, after all. But I said nothing. I just sat in my chair, choking back my anger. I felt completely powerless. I assumed that if I complained about Whiteshirt, I would simply be consid- ered "paranoid" or "oversensitive." I could have asked for a transfer to another section; but that, I decided, would look like defeat. Besides, it had been more than eleven months since I'd joined Nation and there was a chance that, at the end of a year, I might be rotated to the back of the book. In the meantime, it seemed that the only thing I could do was to silently loathe Whiteshirt.

Late one Thursday afternoon, Whiteshirt summoned me to his office. He assigned me a story on state budget surpluses around the country; in a change of pace, he, not Minuteman, would edit my piece. Whiteshirt told me to emphasize the ingenious ways in which governors were tightening their budget belts and increasing state coffers. I suggested that the point of the story should be how Rea- gan's proposed federal budget cuts would force the states to cover financial needs that had traditionally been met by the U.S. government. Most governors were arguing that Reagan's cuts would wipe out their state reserves in one swoop. "That's where the tension in the story is," I said. "Maybe we should approach it from that angle."

"No," Whiteshirt said. "The M.E. wants an upbeat story on how frugal these governors are. So let's build the article around that."

"Well," I said, "how about this—"

"Just write it *my* way," he snapped.

That settled it. I wrote the story my way.

As I sat in front of my computer terminal that Thursday night, flagrantly disobeying Whiteshirt's instructions, I knew I might be jeopardizing my career at *Time*. I knew that a stunt like this could damage my reputation among the editors. But I realized something else, something that I felt gave me an edge over the white men in dark suits: I wasn't afraid of them. They spent their lives fearing each other but not one of them could frighten me. And I knew I had my father to thank for that. Dad had scared me so much and for so long that I simply didn't have any fear left for anybody else.

First thing Friday morning, Whiteshirt called me into his office. The famously even-tempered editor was apoplectic. "Why did I waste my breath telling you how to write this story! You just thought you could go out and write what you *think*!" he screamed, his face growing red and puffy. "Your job isn't to write what you *think*! Your job is to write the story *I* tell you to write! Which is what the Managing Editor *wants*!"

At the end of Whiteshirt's tantrum, I shrugged and said I thought my way of writing the story made more sense. He dismissed me from his office and rewrote the piece. I went home that weekend confident that I would soon be expelled from the Nation section.

But months passed and I wasn't transferred. Whiteshirt started treating me with the same respect he showed other staffers. I didn't know what to make of it. Did he respect me because I hadn't capitulated? Or did he just feel better about me now that I'd given him a chance to scream his head off? Maybe, I thought, I should have yelled back at him. Maybe I'd completely misjudged him and he wasn't a racist after all. Then, one day, an unexpected development: Whiteshirt resigned from *Time* and went off to become a top editor at Brand X. Three years later, Whiteshirt so antagonized that magazine's most prominent black correspondent that the reporter left Brand X and defected to *Time.* Another oversensitive paranoid, perhaps.

CHAPTER 8

NEW YORK, 1986. There was a meanness in the air; and an accumulating dread that the melting pot was about to boil over. Ed Koch, the abrasive, race-baiting mayor who was in his ninth year in City Hall and popular as ever despite the corruption that permeated his administration, set the tone for a pissed-off citizenry. And cab drivers, never the most civic-minded of New Yorkers, were more obnoxious than ever. One night my girlfriend Kate and I were walking through SoHo when we got caught in a driving rainstorm. Thunder, lightning, high winds; Wrath of God weather. We stopped at a corner, shivering under the tattered remains of a tiny, cheap umbrella. I stepped into the street and saw a free taxi speeding our way. I hailed it. The cab zoomed right past me. I turned and saw the driver stop for a white couple two blocks up the street. "Fucking pig," I muttered. Kate, still standing on the sidewalk, shrugged. I spotted another cab. I hoped for a black driver but, as the taxi drew near, I saw a young white guy sporting a pompadour behind the wheel. I just knew he was going to pass us. But he seemed to be slowing down. Then I noticed that the traffic light at our corner had turned red. Perfect—the driver would have no choice but to stop and take us. The cab slowed to a halt. I grabbed the handle and started to open the door. At that moment, the light turned

green and the taxi tore up the street. "Asshole!" Kate
hissed. "Maybe I should try?" she asked. For expediency's
sake, I returned to the sidewalk and stood out of the line
of vision of any approaching cabbie while Kate, a tall and
slender white woman, stepped off the curb and extended
her arm. Sure enough, the next free taxi stopped for her.

Following Kate into the cab, I suddenly remembered
my father depositing Ruth around the corner from her office building so her colleagues wouldn't see him. I didn't
know what made me more ashamed: that I had been so
contemptuous of my father for hiding his brown face, or
that, six years later, I was doing the exact same thing. As we
sped uptown, the rain clattering on the roof of the taxi, I
sat silently beside Kate, feeling enraged, and somehow
emasculated. Kate placed her hand on my knee and smiled
reassuringly. "Don't worry about it," she said.

Kate and I had been friends first, then lovers, and as
our relationship grew, we'd become something like allies,
trying to protect each other from life's blows. Since we both
worked at *Time,* we could help each other negotiate the
politics of the place, giving advice on what moves to make
and whom to look out for. Most of all Kate and I loved to
talk. We could banter for hours, always engaging and pro-
voking each other. Kate's pleasant, unassuming demeanor
masked a subversive wit, a keen sense of the absurdity of
people and their social constructs. Our long, rambling conversations, which were, in their way, quietly, powerfully
erotic, had formed the strongest bond between us. Yet, in
the two years we had been together, Kate and I had rarely
talked about race, at least not in terms of our relationship.
This was not, I had believed, because our racial difference
was such a sensitive issue, but because it was simply no big
deal between us. But there were always people eager to

remind us that we were an ugly affront, and a threat, to their world order.

Roy was scaring the neighbors again. Early one evening he dropped by my apartment building, a five-story brownstone on the Upper West Side, entering the vestibule behind one of the other tenants, a ferrety middle-aged white man with a droopy mustache. The man was about to put his key in the door when he turned and saw Roy. The terror flashed in his eyes. He backed into a corner of the vestibule, his body rigid, mouth agape in a silent scream of horror at the sight of this very tall, creamy-coffee-hued young man. "Get a grip," Roy said in his bone-dry baritone as he pressed my buzzer. "I'm not gonna mug you."

I rang Roy in and, as he entered the lobby, my neighbor, still frozen in the corner, croaked, "Thank you."

Roy climbed the steep flights of stairs to my top-floor apartment where we shared a brittle chuckle over the incident. I offered him a Coke and we sat down on the couch, continuing what I often thought of as a single running conversation that we'd begun at age twelve. After college, Roy had stayed in Providence another year, working odd jobs, playing with bands and writing songs, before returning to New York, where he had the hardest job of anyone I knew. Roy was a case worker in Brooklyn, "a shrink for poor people," as he put it. For a grossly inadequate salary, he counseled families coping with all varieties of personal anguish. I admired Roy for the social conviction and self-lessness that I lacked. What I found hard to believe was that Roy, in turn, admired me for succeeding in a place like *Time*.

Things were going well for me at work. Finally out of Whiteshirt's shadow, Minuteman had become chief senior editor of the Nation section in 1985. "We'd like you to be more a part of the team," Minuteman told me shortly after taking over the section. I knew that when he said "we" he meant "I" and when he talked about "the team" he meant that he had appointed himself as my mentor and I should behave more like a loyal protégé. The problem was that after nearly two years in Nation, I was still looking for a chance to move to the back of the book. But my competitive streak kept me from requesting a transfer. I figured if I was going to write for *Time* magazine, I might as well work in the toughest section with the highest profile. So I did my best to be a "team player."

Minuteman assigned me more of Nation's lead stories on Reagan administration policy, congressional battles and important elections. And though I often cringed at the rightward slant my stories were given by the top editors, I continued to write them. There were many articles that I later wished my byline had not appeared on, but the sheer kick of seeing my byline in *Time* magazine every week numbed the pain. Because Minuteman never ordered me to write a story a certain way, and because he favored that pro-and-con structure that sometimes obscured the articles' conservative tinge, I could tell myself I was producing good, balanced pieces. To get them a bit more balanced, I often made subtle changes on my stories on Saturday mornings when Minuteman usually wasn't in the office, deleting an adjective here, adding a qualifier there, shifting the pieces slightly more to the left.

One week I received a furious letter from a right-wing activist accusing me of a liberal bias in my articles. I was thrilled. Adding to my excitement was the fact that if this man knew me, he'd be even more horrified that I was writing for *Time* magazine. I must have been his nightmare journalist: a black, New York–bred twenty-five-year-old with a "secular humanist" high school education, a degree from the paragon of Ivy League elitism and a white girl-friend. The only thing that might have disgusted him more was if I had a white boyfriend.

After a while, I forgot about moving to the back of the book. I received handsome raises and pats on the back from my colleagues. My mother could show the magazine to her friends at the office and boast about her son's success. And, somewhere in the back of my mind, I hoped my father was reading my articles. Every success I achieved was a measure of revenge against him. I would show him that I *did* have marketable skills, that I *could* make it without him: *See, Dad! Hah! Aren't you sorry now? Aren't you proud of me? Don't you love me?*

But *Time* magazine for me, like social work for Roy, was often just a job, something peripheral to more consuming creative endeavors. Roy was still composing prolifically, taping songs on his four-track recorder. He always played his new tunes for me and was, at the time, getting ready to go into the studio and put together his first demo tape. I, meanwhile, was writing in fits and starts, struggling to complete a very bad attempt at a play. It was emotionally taxing work. I knew that the writing was leading me to the core of my relationship with my father and our lives as black men. I wasn't entirely sure I wanted to go there.

"Damn, he's an ugly fuck," Roy said as we sat on my couch watching a young British pop singer with a bloated face and flaming red hair on MTV.

"A real Howdy Doody," I said of the fellow trying desperately to sound like Aretha Franklin as he shrieked through a song that seemed derived from an old O'Jays hit. Like so many white performers on the music video channel, he was backed up by a trio of black female singers who did their best to lend his soul a modicum of credibility. I thought of a word I'd been hearing a lot lately, usually applied by black people to other blacks who seemed too eager to assimilate: "wannabe," as in wanting to be white. But it had always seemed to me that there were far more white people who wanted to be black than vice versa. And the only person *I* could ever remember wanting to be was Dr. J., the basketball genius who, so far as I knew, had always been black.

The video ended and a beer commercial appeared on the screen. "Just as proud as the people who are drinkin' it today," voices on the soundtrack warbled as various images of macho white men—motorcycle cops, guys in cowboy hats and pickup trucks—flashed by in rapid succession, "Miller's made the American way!"

"Christ," Roy said. "What do they want you to think, that Budweiser's brewed in Leningrad?"

Next we were treated to a commercial for a new movie, something about squinty-eyed, clean-shaven American teens who managed to get themselves trapped behind the Iron Curtain. The commercial ended with one of the cornfed young lads firing an automatic weapon wildly and screaming, "Die, you Russian murderers!" The film's title appeared: *Born American.*

"Born to kill Commies!" I barked.

"Born to spill the blood of Reds!" Roy snarled in response.

We laughed archly, knowing that we lived in an era of mindless jingoism, a time when the word "American" seemed the exclusive property of Reagan and his ilk. And whatever an "American" was in their context, the term clearly did not encompass folks like Roy and me. At the

same time, the term African American was coming into
vogue among a lot of black people. I liked the expression
and would eventually start using it in my *Time* articles whenever I could. But while Africa was in my genes, in traditions,
attitudes, modes of expression that were known and un-
known to me, Africa itself was an abstraction, a place I'd
never been and had seen only in books and films. America,
in fact, was the only country I'd ever really known. Except
for a brief weekend trip to Montreal when I was thirteen,
I'd never set foot outside the United States. It had been
centuries since my purely African ancestors were dragged
over here in chains, long before the biggest waves of willing
European, Scandinavian, Hispanic and Asian immigrants
arrived on these shores. And one of my great-great-grand-
fathers was Cherokee. Whether anybody liked it or not, I
was about as American as one could be.

I turned off the television and Roy and I headed out for
some dinner. We walked west toward Broadway, to a dark,
woody bar we liked. I generally avoided Columbus Avenue,
the popular thoroughfare just east of my apartment building. When I was eleven years old and first started venturing
into Manhattan alone, Columbus was little more than a
bleak strip of tenements. With the initial burst of yuppie
gentrification in the late seventies, the avenue was transformed into a neighborhood of funky restaurants, cozy bars
and street musicians, a sort of uptown Greenwich Village.
This was still my image of the area when a good friend from
college left New York to attend graduate school and asked
me if I'd like to take over the lease on his apartment at 74th
and Columbus. Once I moved in, I found that most of the
funky hangouts had been usurped by ultrachic boutiques;
the unpretentious restaurants had turned expensive and
glitzy. The used-book store my cousin Asa and I had fre-

quented as teenagers had been replaced by a shop selling pricey, pointless tchochkes, the former proprietor forced to peddle his books on corners with the other street vendors who lined Columbus, hawking jewelry and hats, T-shirts and fake Rolex watches. Where street performers had once entertained the crowds, panhandlers now mingled among the hordes of consumers, bumming for quarters.

Roy and I used to argue about whether one should give money to the panhandlers. Roy never did, saying they would only use it to buy crack or booze or heroin. Besides, he sometimes remarked, "I gave at the office," meaning he did his share for the poor every day at work. But I didn't give at the office. I gave to my brother Bert, helping to put him through college; and occasionally I gave to the Salvation Army. But when confronted by a beggar on the street, I often felt a frisson of guilt and forked over whatever change I had in my pocket.

At times, I thought the guilt must have been plain on my face, making me an easy mark for street people seeking charity. I liked to walk the mile and a half from my apartment to the Time-Life Building and, on most mornings, would be accosted about every other block. Once, a young panhandler standing on the corner of 57th and Seventh called out as he spotted me coming. "Yo, black man, can you help a brother out?" It was the first time I'd heard such a blatantly racial pitch. I stopped at the corner, waiting for the light to change. The panhandler stood beside me. "Yo, blood, can you help me out? I'm tryin' a get my life together, I swear I'm tryin', just a quarter, man, that's all I'm axin you for." He wore a black warm-up suit and a red baseball cap turned backward; the whites of his eyes were yellow. "Please," he said. "Brother." I fished in my pocket and came up with two quarters. The panhandler stared at the money in his palm. "Fifty cent," he said flatly. I felt an urge to apologize, to explain that I didn't have any more change. I was on the verge of offering him a dollar bill when he looked up and said, "God bless you, brother," and walked away.

Crossing the street, I wondered about the young man who was my exact height and build, looked about my age, and had probably been born in the same town, and I thought, Now, really, what is the difference between him and me? It occurred to me that my father would have gotten a hoot out of that question. "What's the difference?" Dad would have said in mock amazement. "I'll tell you what the difference is: *you've* got money!" My father didn't believe in luck. Sometimes, luck was the only thing I did believe in.

I was sitting in front of my computer terminal late one Thursday night, writing another Washington policy story, when Minuteman called me into his office. He was hanging a suit bag on the back of his door when I came in. "Hey, bro," he said cheerfully.

Bro? The word clanged as it left his lips, giving me that queasy feeling I always got when white people tried to talk "black" to me.

Figuring there was a tuxedo in the bag, I asked Minuteman what he'd been up to that evening.

"Just a black tie dinner," he said. He paused and focused his huge eyes on me expectantly.

"Oh," I said.

"A black tie dinner at the Harvard Club," he added, then paused again.

"Oh."

"A board of directors dinner."

"Really."

Minuteman sat behind his desk and gave me a quizzical look. "You're not a member of the Harvard Club are you?"

"No."

He leaned forward and in a suggestive, vaguely conspiratorial tone, asked, "Do you wanna be?" He seemed to be hinting that he could pull some strings to get me in, an odd implication since all one had to do to join the Harvard Club was graduate from Harvard and pay membership dues.

"No," I said, "I don't really like clubs."

Minuteman straightened up, startled and suddenly uncertain. "Oh, yeah, well, neither do I really. I mean, I just used to go to the club to play squash and I just, kind of, wound up on the board of directors."

"Uh-huh."

Then he got to his point. Minuteman felt the magazine had been ignoring social problems. He wanted Nation to run more stories on "race and poverty issues," life in the ghetto, social policy, the "underclass." He wanted to know if I'd be interested in writing some of these stories. "I think you could bring a vital point of view to these pieces," he said earnestly.

I squirmed slightly in my chair. The few "race and poverty" articles *Time* had run in recent years had been essentially horror stories focusing on alarming incidents of crime and senseless violence among young black men in the inner city, sensational stories typically illustrated with harsh black-and-white photos and written in a hyped-up tone of anxiety and indignation, stories that seemed designed primarily to frighten white readers. I also bridled at the term "underclass." I'd first heard the expression used by a black sociologist and liked the way it evoked America's system of both class and caste. But it was rapidly becoming a code word that white media pundits, from the sputtering right-wingers to the mealy-mouthed liberals, could use to define that repugnant Other. "Underclass" put a sociological patina on the us-versus-them rhetoric that passed for political debate. Instead of condemning Ronald Reagan's "welfare queens" and "young bucks," the sophisticated bigot decried the "underclass." I could tell Minuteman liked using the word, not out of any prejudice but simply because it was a hot, new catchphrase.

"Frankly," I said, "I haven't really liked the race and poverty stories I've read in the magazine."

"Sure," Minuteman said quickly, "but I didn't edit any of those stories and I will be editing these. And I will fight to make sure that these will be fair, balanced stories."

"Really."

"Of course. I mean, I care, very deeply, about these issues. I think when it comes to civil rights and that sort of thing, you and I are probably very much on the same wavelength politically."

"You think so?"

"Absolutely. I care very deeply about these issues. You probably couldn't find another editor in this building who cares about these issues as deeply as I do."

Alas, I didn't doubt it. But I was, at this point, the only African American writer in the New York office. There had recently been three of us, but one had returned to the newspaper where she'd begun her career and the other had quit journalism to return to his first profession, law. As the lone black writer, I was particularly wary of being used.

I felt a shudder of déjà vu. Years earlier, the very week I joined the *Crimson,* the paper became embroiled in a racial controversy. To illustrate a story on the prison system, an editor pulled a photo of two young black men out of the picture file and superimposed cell bars over their faces. The two men in the photo—whom the editor said he considered "scruffy-looking" enough to pass for convicts—were, in fact, Harvard students. There were threats of a lawsuit, a demonstration by black students outside the *Crimson* office, a long editorial apologizing for the newspaper's "unconscious racism." While I never defended my colleagues for the gaffe, some friends still criticized me for working on the paper. A year later, one of the *Crimson*'s top editors took me out to dinner to persuade me to run for the office of editorial chairman. After an hour of his cajoling, I still wasn't sure I wanted the job. Then, he said, "Think of what it would mean to other black students." It was a clumsy ploy, since I felt certain that the editor's main concern was what my election would mean to the *Crimson*: a black editor whose position near the top of the masthead could be pointed to next time the paper was caught being "unconsciously racist." I decided not to run.

"So," Minuteman said, "what do you say?"

"Let me think about it awhile," I answered.

"Sure thing, chief," he said with a wink.

Survivor was in town and wanted to take me out to lunch. Survivor had started his career on an underground black newspaper in the late sixties. By the mid-eighties, he was *Time* magazine's Chicago bureau chief. I liked Survivor because he was a remarkably thorough and incisive reporter whose files always made for a good read. But what I liked even more was that Survivor didn't take a lot of shit. If *Time* covered black issues at all, it was mainly because Survivor kept the pressure on the top editors to do it. And if those stories had any shred of liberalism in them it was because

Survivor battled over every line of the articles he reported, making sure that at least some hint of his own point of view made it into the magazine. Though the editors had the final say, they usually made concessions to Survivor just to end his barrage of phone calls and computer messages to the New York office. And, of course, the *Time* brass was always pleased to picture their star black correspondent in the Letter from the Publisher, showing the public that they were doing their bit for racial equality. A former staff writer, Survivor was an accomplished infighter; but he preferred the relative autonomy of being out in the field to the bureaucratic brawls of the Big House in Manhattan. What Survivor needed was a surrogate, a real ally in the New York office, someone he could work with in tandem to see that his stories ran the way he wanted them to. And so we had lunch.

Survivor had a point-blank directness that knocked people off balance (during the 1984 vice-presidential debate he completely flummoxed George Bush simply by looking him in the eye and asking him about his record on civil rights). "So," he inquired before our appetizers had arrived, "why are you a journalist?"

"Because I like to write and it pays the bills," I answered, attempting to sound hard-boiled. "Why are *you* a journalist?"

"To tell the story of black America." Survivor squinted at me as he took a long drag on his cigarette. He exhaled slowly. "That's the number one reason and the only really important one as far as I'm concerned. To tell the story of black America—fairly, honestly, and with integrity."

"Do you think you get to do that in *Time*?"

Survivor shrugged. "It's a struggle. But if we don't try to do it, who will?"

Nobody I could think of.

．　．　．

It was to be my first cover story, a piece slugged "Under-class Families," examining how fatherless households helped perpetuate the cycle of poverty in the inner city. I was iffy on the subject. With families all over America—black and white, rich, poor, and in-between—falling to pieces, I wondered if paternal negligence was a legitimate focus for the article or just another twisted example of how "social pathology" was the main cause of black poverty. Survivor understood my reservations but argued that we would, in this story, analyze the broad forces at work on the black poor. "We're going to talk about it all," he said in his rapid-fire style, proceeding to count off points on his fingers. "We're going to talk about the decline of manufacturing in the U.S. and the subsequent loss of jobs for working-class black people, the result being a dearth of wage-earning young black men who can afford to support a family once they get their girlfriends pregnant. We're going to talk about the migration of well-to-do blacks out of the ghetto after the civil rights movement which resulted in a lack of good role models for black children within their communities. We're going to talk about Reagan's devastating cuts in job programs that benefited the poor. We're going to cut through all the neocon bullshit and tell the truth." Sounded pretty good to me.

Correspondents around the country were excited by the chance to report on the serious social problems that *Time* generally gave short shrift to. They all sent excellent reports for the article, though Survivor's files from Chicago dominated the piece. The writing went smoothly. I was basically just a middle man, trying to balance Survivor's emphasis on vast societal forces with Minuteman's desire to focus on personal responsibility. I turned in a draft to the Nation editor on a Wednesday night. Without much distortion, Minuteman edited the story and sent it on to the top editors. On Thursday night, I stood in Minuteman's office with Player, looking at the photo that would appear on the cover: an austere portrait of a young black mother and her two children. The Managing Editor smiled. "I'm really glad we're getting this story in the magazine," he said. I went home that night feeling satisfied and a bit virtuous. In some small way, I thought, I had helped tell the story of black America.

The next morning I was sitting at my desk, sipping a cup of coffee when Lifer appeared in my doorway. "The system sucks," he said with a wry half smile. I asked him what he meant. His face shut down. "Oh, jeez, you mean you haven't heard?" The cover story, he said, had been postponed indefinitely—a de facto death sentence.

I rushed into Minuteman's office. He sat behind his desk looking pale and exhausted. "I was just about to come down and tell you."

Player and the top editors had decided early Friday morning that our article was appearing too soon after a cover on teen pregnancy, also edited by Minuteman, that had run three months earlier. Why then, I asked, had they not set a rescheduling date instead of effectively killing our story with this indefinite postponement? Besides, *Time* had run cover stories on two right-wing television evangelists, Jerry Falwell and Pat Robertson, just two months apart. Weren't the top editors concerned about the similarities between those two articles? And our story had been in the works for several weeks, a draft of it had been in the computer for any editorial staffer to read for two days. Why did it take the top editors until the day before closing to decide

not to run it? Why did Player tell me he was glad to be
getting the story in the magazine, then turn around and kill
it twelve hours later? Minuteman didn't have any answers.

Throughout the morning, I heard from staffers who
had been privy to the top editors' discussions of the article.
Looking at photos to illustrate the piece, some editors complained that the women and children in the pictures "didn't
look poor enough." Paradoxically, they argued that poverty
was a downer and no one wanted to read about it anymore.
There was also a squeamishness about running too many
black faces on the cover of *Time*—even the visages of the
rich and famous. Once when an editor suggested a cover on
Whitney Houston, another editor replied, "We just had
Dwight Gooden on the cover three months ago." Then
there was the Editor-in-Chief. It was speculated that the
Baron had never liked the idea of running our story and
may have waited until Friday morning to order it perma-
nently shelved.

That afternoon I wandered around midtown in the
rain. I veered between feeling that I'd been screwed by the
powers that be and worrying that maybe I'd ruined a good
story by not writing as well as I could have. I contemplated
quitting my job. But I was still spooning my way out of a
grave of debt. And there was Bert to think about—he relied
on me for a good deal of financial support. And where else
would I work? Maybe, I thought, I should just abandon
writing altogether.

I was mentally drafting my letter of resignation when
I returned to the office and found Survivor walking up and
down the Nation corridor, looking for me.

"Jake," he said, putting an arm around my shoulders,
"I flew in from Chicago as soon as I got the news. You're
mad, right? You sure look mad."

"Of course I'm mad. Aren't you?"

"You know what they say. Don't get mad. Get even."

"How?"

"We're going to come right back at 'em. They don't want to do a story on underclass women and children, fine. We'll just turn the tables on them, shift the emphasis of the piece. We'll do a cover on the crisis of young black men in the ghetto. We'll make the exact same points we made in this story, we'll just focus on the men. I've already got a slug: we'll call it 'Native Sons.'"

"Oh, come on, that's the same wild-in-the-streets ghetto story *Time* always runs."

"Not the way we're going to do it. 'Native Sons' will be different, smarter, more analytical."

"I don't know. I'm sick of banging my head against a wall. Besides, 'Native Sons'? I'm not sure I'm ready to characterize an entire generation of men as latter-day Bigger Thomases."

"Hey, man, a lot of them *are* latter-day Bigger Thomases. Do you want to salvage this cover or not?"

We went to Minuteman's office and Survivor pitched the idea to him. Minuteman liked it, as I knew he would. Native Sons. What a catchphrase.

Nine months had passed since the killing of "Underclass Families." Correspondents had geared up for "Native Sons" and once again sent good, scrupulous files. And once again, Survivor's work set the tone for the piece I wrote. Weeks after I finished a draft of "Native Sons," the top editors still refused to schedule a date for it to run. But Minuteman kept pushing for it. Finally, Player and his minions gave us the green light. But they would not run the story as a cover. They would publish the piece at half its original length as an inside feature. "It's the best we're gonna get," Minuteman said, "so we might as well go for it."

Following an ancient formula, I led off the article with the personal story of one of the "Native Sons," a biographical sketch outlining the broader points of the piece, written in traditional Timese:

"At 23, John Deryl Scott is a shy, thoughtful young man with simple aspirations. 'I want to live a family life,' says he, 'have a nice job, have a nice car, do fine things in life, take vacations.' Though he says he is 'rather hopeful' about the future, the odds are against him. Three years ago, he was charged with taking part in the robbery of a Detroit car wash that resulted in the shooting death of the owner. While Scott was not accused of pulling the trigger, a jury nonetheless convicted him of first-degree murder. He is currently serving a life sentence in a correctional facility in western Michigan.

" 'I guess you could say that I was not dealt a nice hand in life,' says Scott. He lived with his mother who supported her children on a monthly welfare check and food stamps until he was placed in a youth home at age eight; he has seen his father only a handful of times. By 16, Scott was an unemployed, unmarried father, running with a Detroit street gang. A year later, he was shot in the chest after refusing to give his fancy leather jacket to three other youths.

"In the three years since his conviction, Scott has been a model prisoner, earning his high school equivalency degree and tutoring other inmates. His attorney has filed for a new trial and Scott prays that someday he will be released and reunited with his young daughter. When asked about his old friends from the neighborhood, Scott replies: 'Most of the young men I grew up with are dead, incarcerated or born-again Christians. A few select ones had people in places who helped them get nice jobs. But a lot of black kids don't have that kind of opportunity.' "

Minuteman and Survivor both felt the story needed a more dramatic opening, and urged me to write a sketch reported by a West Coast correspondent:

" 'The only thing I did in high school every day was fight and shoot,' says 27-year-old Booker Cole, with an air of bravado. 'There was a time when people wouldn't talk to me because I would either beat them up or "smoke" them if I didn't like what they said.' A member of one of Los Angeles's biggest black street gang networks since he was ten, Cole has served time for robbery and cocaine dealing. Now he is back in jail after being sentenced last May to serve six years for assault with a deadly weapon. 'Death is a part of living,' says he. 'The only thing I can do is strap two .44s on my chest, keep an Uzi under the seat and a .45 in my hand. If they're going to get me, I'll take some of them with me.' "

Scott's story, meanwhile, was boiled down to a caption that would appear under his photograph:

"Johnnie Deryl Scott, 23, is serving a life sentence for taking part in the robbery of a Detroit car wash that resulted in the murder of the owner. He is seeking a new trial, and hopes someday to be reunited with the daughter he fathered out of wedlock six years ago.

" 'The young men I grew up with are dead, incarcerated or born-again Christians. A few . . . got nice jobs. But a lot of black kids don't have that opportunity.' "

The photo that accompanied this truncated profile was of a stone-faced Scott standing in front of a barbed-wire fence. The other pictures illustrating the piece showed menacing-looking young black men shot against such stark backgrounds as a graffiti-covered cement wall. I complained to Survivor that the photos and the Booker Cole lead undermined the serious substance of the article. "Look, Jake," he said, "just getting this story in the magazine at all is a victory."

Though the editors had delayed running the story and refused to feature it on the cover, they nevertheless wanted a picture of *Time*'s one and only black writer in the Letter from the Publisher. I gave the staff writer who interviewed me for the Publetter precisely the sort of quote she was looking for: working on "Native Sons," I said, "I was reminded that I was fortunate to grow up in a two-parent home and have access to a good education."

After the interview, I winced at what a fatuous line I had given the writer. But then, I thought, it was true, wasn't it? I *had* been lucky to go to Fieldston and Harvard. And though I could hardly bear even to think about my father sometimes, he had given me the tools and the support I needed to make my way in the world. After all, what sort of model had he had? He never saw his own father after age thirteen. Had Dad really done such a terrible job? Deciding it was better not to think about it, I quickly shut my father out of my mind again.

Just as I had decided my Publetter quote was not completely banal, I got a look at the photo that would run with the column. There I was, clean-cut, smiling, looking like the quintessential bourgeois Negro, in a crisp, brilliantly white button-down shirt. Juxtaposed with the photos of John Deryl Scott and the others, I felt as if I had been set up as some sort of "nonthreatening" alternative to those nasty "Native Sons." Looking at the magazine Monday morning, I almost wished the article had never run.

Then came the response to the story. I received a score of letters from African American readers, nearly all of their comments favorable. Apparently unfazed by the story's sensational aspects, the readers seemed happy that black issues were being given at least some serious treatment in *Time* magazine. Relieved, I could consider myself a virtuous journalist again. Until I got a letter from a reader in western Michigan, and felt the stab of shame like a knife in the belly:

Dear Mr. Lamar:

The picture of me and the article of "Today's Native Sons" leaves out one thing—HOPE.
    After being in prison for 3 years I have had enough hope to get my G.E.D., to be a Chapel assistant, to be a full-time Instructor aide, and a Chairman in the N.A.A.C.P. If I can still have hope, then the *Time* article should be able to show hope.

        Thank you for your time,
            Johnnie D. Scott

Minuteman assigned me to a catchall story on "life in the ghetto." I declined to write it. He assigned me a story on welfare reform. I turned it down. Refusing to work on two different stories was not an option *Time* staff writers generally exercised. Minuteman responded by virtually ostracizing me for several weeks and assigning me only brief one- and two-column stories. But with the Iran-contra scandal dominating the news during much of 1987, he couldn't keep any decent Nation writer in his doghouse for long, and I was soon cranking out big stories again. I did my work reliably, racked up a few cover stories, and was promoted to associate editor. But whatever enthusiasm I'd had for the job was gone.

Survivor moved back to New York and became the first black senior editor in the magazine's history. He called me into his office one afternoon to tell me he was trying to convince the top editors to schedule a cover on the black middle class. He wanted me to write it.

"No way," I said.

"Now, Jake, this isn't another ghetto story."

"Right. *Time* won't run a cover on the underclass, but the middle class is okay?"

"You just don't want to be typecast," he said with a sneer.

"The issue isn't typecasting. The issue is fairness."

"The story will be fair. *I'm* going to edit this piece. I'll make sure that the story runs the way we want it to."

"And what if you and I disagree?"

"We won't disagree."

"How do you know?"

"I'm sure we could work out any differences . . ."

"Forget it. I let these guys use me before. I'm not gonna let it happen again."

"How did anybody *use* you?"

"They fucked us over on two cover stories and then ran my picture in the Publetter like they're so progressive."

"But that is progress. A black man writing important stories for *Time* magazine. That's progress!"

"I've been the only black writer at this magazine for two years. What kind of progress is that?"

"We're working on that. We're going to have more black writers here soon."

"Well, good luck. You've got sixty-five years of institutional racism working against you."

Survivor stared at me appraisingly and leaned back in his chair. "I don't know what you were expecting when you came out of Harvard."

"I don't know either," I heard myself mumble.

"It's like I tell my two sons," Survivor said, putting his feet up on his desk. "Racism is there. Racism is always going to be there. Racism is like hurricanes. If you live in a place where there are hurricanes, you can sit around wringing your hands and crying about how the hurricanes are going to wipe you out, or you can take the proper precautions, fortify your house, take intelligent steps to defend yourself against the hurricanes."

"Or," I said, "you can move."

Survivor's eyes narrowed. "Well," he said quietly, "I know how you feel. But it's easy to just up and run away. Sometimes it takes more guts to stay and fight the good fight."

"Yeah," I said, turning to the door, "well, I got a story to write."

"Besides," he said, "where are you going to go where there *isn't* racism?" Survivor let out a short, hard laugh. "Huh? Where do you think you're gonna go?"

CHAPTER 9

I HATED SLEEPING ALONE. By myself, it usually took a good two hours of reading in bed or staring at the ceiling before I could fall asleep. Once I finally did drift off, I slept the fitful three-quarters sleep of my childhood, as if I were still on alert for the sound of my father's key in the door. I usually woke up just before dawn, startled by some vivid dream. Then another hour or so would pass before I fell back asleep. After I'd at last surrendered to a comfortable snooze, the alarm clock would go off, time to get up. Only with a woman's warm body beside me could I sleep peacefully.

But by the summer of 1988, I was getting used to late-night solitude. A year and a half had passed since I'd broken up with Kate. Though I'd been involved with a few other women since my relationship with Kate ended, I hadn't stayed with any of them for very long. As lonely as I was without a woman, I felt much lonelier when I was with a woman I didn't love. I had loved Kate, and sometimes I'd wanted urgently to go back to her. I couldn't do it though, and after eighteen months, I was almost convinced that breaking up really had been the right thing to do.

Kate and I would meet for dinner once in a while, trying to keep our friendship alive. But we found it difficult to talk for very long without somehow hurting each other.

I would search for a way to tell her how much our three years together had meant to me, but she always let me know she didn't want to hear any eulogies for our failed relationship. Inevitably, we would lapse into the Recriminations Hour. I would criticize her for being too insecure, too demanding. She would tell me why I had been a lousy boyfriend, that I was too self-absorbed, too noncommittal.

"You know," Kate said one night as we sat in what had been our favorite Italian restaurant, reexamining the wreckage of our romance, "sometimes I can't help thinking your breaking up with me was a failure of nerve."

She was right. The more I'd grown to rely on Kate, the more anxious I'd become about the intensity of our relationship. Kate was thirty years old when we broke up, and thinking seriously about marriage. I was twenty-five and terrified by the very idea. Marriage seemed, at best, a life of crushing tedium, an endless procession of chores and bills and petty squabbles. For marriage at its worst, or the worst I could envision, I had only to look to my parents. I had an almost superstitious dread of marriage, a feeling that, as soon as I uttered my wedding vows, I would turn into my father.

In the years since I'd last spoken to Dad, I'd been able to acknowledge that there was much goodness in him. The problem was that the good and the bad were so intertwined. Despite the positive qualities I'd received from him—his confidence, his perseverance—I knew I'd inherited negative traits as well. But I wanted to keep those bad qualities—whatever they might be—under lock and key; to defeat them by denying them. My fear was that once I got married, the badness would come roaring to the surface. I felt that my father had damaged me in innumerable ways and I didn't want to damage any children of my own. Everyone said that, of course, that they didn't want to make the same mistakes their parents had made, but everyone seemed to go ahead and make them anyway, in one guise or another. Dad's father had dropped out of his life when he was thirteen; my father had disappeared from my life when I was twenty-two. Dad, I believed, had fulfilled his most important goal as a parent: he had been a better father to his children than his father had been to him. But whatever good my father had done, I couldn't get past his violence. I felt certain that I didn't have my father's capacity for physical violence; but his emotional violence had left its share of scars. I worried about what sort of emotional violence I might be capable of. If I was going to have to live with the pain of the past, I thought, better to bear it by myself alone than to inflict it on my innocent children. Kate told me it didn't have to be that way, that you didn't have to hurt your children as you had been hurt. Sometimes I believed her. But, on the whole, I thought it wiser not to take the risk.

"It's true," I said to Kate across the dim, candle-lit table. "A commitment like marriage, that takes a lot of nerve."

"I mean the nerve to marry a white woman."

I felt as if someone had dropped an ice cube down my spine. "I don't think so," I said. "I think my problems, our problems, have more to do with, you know, intimacy and commitment than with, uh, race or culture."

"Maybe," Kate said.

"I don't know."

But I did know; or, perhaps more accurately, I was beginning to find out.

There had been no racial hassles with Kate's New England Yankee family. Kate's parents were comfortable with themselves and comfortable with me and Kate said her folks would like to see us married. I wasn't sure I could say the same for my mother. Mom had met Kate and liked her. She had, in fact, never objected to any woman I'd been involved with. But when it came to the general topic of black men with white women, Mom never hesitated to make her feelings known. She kept a mental shit list of black celebrities who had white wives or girlfriends. When a woman she knew married a white man, my mother was pleased; but when a male acquaintance married a white woman, she criticized him at every turn. It seemed inconceivable to Mom that a black man might fall genuinely in love with a white woman; he could only be with her *because* she was white. "It's just as easy to fall in love with a black girl," Mom once said. This, I thought, was precisely the point: it *was* just as easy for me; it all depended on the girl.

Of course, Mom was careful to maintain, she would be happy with any woman I decided to marry. But sometimes when I contemplated marriage to Kate, I could hear, in the back of my mind, my mother talking on the phone with one of her friends: "Jakie turned out just like his father."

During my last year with Kate, the two of us attracted more and more hostile responses when we walked down the street. Since high school, I'd noticed two kinds of looks from strangers when out with a white date. The most common was the look of curiosity, a mildly inquisitive, puzzled look one might give some garishly costumed pedestrian. The second look was a glare of sheer disgust. It was a stare which, like the more innocuous type, I had received from all kinds of people, male and female, black and white. But, in my mid-twenties, I noticed it coming most frequently and harshly from black women. Sometimes when Kate and I passed a black woman on the street, the stranger might sigh in exasperation or suck her teeth scornfully. One afternoon in a movie theater, a young black woman and her daughter sat in the row behind Kate and me. Throughout the film, I heard the woman muttering under her breath. Though I couldn't make out all the words, I knew she was talking about me. As the closing credits rolled, the little girl, who didn't look much older than four, leaned forward and whispered in my ear: "Dummy."

Sometimes I wanted to walk up to the women and say, "Look, maybe I don't think the way you think I think. You know nothing of what there is between Kate and me. Maybe we just love each other. Is that so hard to believe?" But I didn't talk to strangers. And much as I tried to ignore the low-wave public censure, the hostility took its toll. It made me feel guilty, like a traitor to my race. I wondered if maybe the truly responsible thing to do was to date black women exclusively, to allow myself to fall in love only with black women, to reject love if I found it in a woman who happened to be white. Those thoughts had not been foremost in my mind when I broke up with Kate. But, now that she mentioned it, I had to wonder if I was more of a coward, or a bigot, than I'd thought I was.

The Recriminations Hour was drawing to a close. Kate started talking about her new boyfriend. He was someone she'd gone out with years earlier, and after being reunited for several months they were getting serious. She told me about taking Jim to a beach she and I used to visit. "We were looking for a good spot," Kate said, "and I kept thinking, 'Something's different here, something's weird.' Like there was some aspect of being at the beach that seemed . . . I don't know . . . absent. Then I realized what it was: nobody was staring at us."

I laughed. "That must have been a relief."

"Actually, I kind of missed it."

Try as I might to suppress the past, memories of my father came rushing back like bad dreams. Usually, I'd tell myself I didn't give a damn about Dad or what he thought of me. Other times, I felt an almost desperate need for his approval, his sponsorship in the world. Then, I'd decide I didn't want his emotional support. Just an acknowledgment. I just wanted him to recognize me, to say, Yes, you are my son, you do exist. I thought of the difficulties I had had as a black man in white society, and felt a new awareness of just how hard my father's life must have been. But then the anger I felt toward him would return, more powerful than ever. Alone at night, in my small apartment, I began to feel abstracted from my own life. Haunted by my father, I was becoming a ghost to myself.

Every once in a while, I'd receive a bit of information about Dad, passed through a grapevine of cousins and old family acquaintances who had run into him. I heard he was teaching again, that he was living with a new girlfriend, a nurse, in Yonkers. Bert tracked Dad down and spent an afternoon with him. He said Dad was drinking heavily and seemed depressed.

"Good," I said. "He's caused enough pain for other people, it's time he tasted some himself."

"Don't you ever want to see him again?" Bert asked.

"No."

"He's still our father, Jake."

"He doesn't act like it. He's the one who abandoned *us*, Bert. It was just too easy for him to walk away and drop us all. I can't forgive that."

"I wish you could."

"Well, I can't. And you shouldn't either."

The next time Bert called Dad, the woman he lived with answered the phone. She said she'd see if he was home. Bert could hear Dad in the background: "No, I don't want to talk to him. I can't be bothered with this crap. Tell him I'm not here."

My grandmother had seen her son only twice in the space of five years. The last time he visited, Good gave him a plastic bag filled with greeting cards she had signed and sealed, cards commemorating his last several birthdays and all the Christmases and Father's Days that had passed since they'd last seen each other. "Why did you do this?" my father asked.

"You know I like to give cards," Good said, "but I didn't know where to mail them, so I figured I'd just give them to you next time I saw you."

Later, as he rose to leave, Dad said, "You know I still love you, don't you?"

My grandmother laughed. "I know you do," she said, "in your own selfish way."

Felicia held a party for my grandmother's seventy-fifth birthday. Good received congratulations from friends and relatives all across the country. She heard from every important person in her life, except her only child. "I'm not mad at him, sugar," my grandmother said, glassy-eyed. "I'm not bitter. And I hope you won't be either. That'll only hurt yourself. You can't hold it in your heart."

My sister sent Dad a note taking him to task for not being more attentive to his mother. My father wrote back to her saying, "What you or anybody else thinks of me means about as much to me as a speck of fly shit on an elephant's ass."

. . .

I am sitting in my office in the Nation corridor. I have a cover story to write but I don't know what the subject is. It is well past midnight and I'm the only one on the floor. What's worse, there seems to have been some sort of power failure. I grope around my office in the dark, pick up the phone and dial the number of a researcher. I want to know if she is gathering some background material on the story. She says she's too busy to help. "You don't understand!" I cry. "This is very important. This is a cover story for *Time* magazine!" She tells me I'll have to wait my turn and hangs up.

I phone Kate, but get only her answering machine.

My mother calls. Her arthritis is flaring up. Couldn't I please come to the Bronx right away and sit with her?

"Mom," I say, "I'm writing a cover story. I can't leave now."

"But, Jakie, I need your help."

"I am helping you, Mom. Don't you think my work helps?"

"Jakie, I need you."

Suddenly, my chair has grown large. My feet dangle above the floor. I am wearing pajamas, something I haven't done in fifteen years. And my father is coming down the darkened Nation corridor. I can not hear him, but I feel him. What does he want? He's only a few yards away now. What do you want from me? He's coming right up to my door . . . Daddy? . . .

Alarms sound, clanging, deafening, exploding inside my head. I bolt upright, turning left and right, trying to get my bearings. My pillow is sopping. I look at the clock: still ten minutes before I have to get up for work. Then—the nerve-jangling rattle again. I stumble into the living room and pick up the phone. "Hello?"

"Good morning. Is this Jacob Lamar?"

"Yes."

"Jacob Lamar, *junior*?"

"Yeah."

"Actually, it's Jacob Lamar *senior* I need to speak with. Could you tell me how to locate him?"

"Who are you?"

"I'm a private investigator and I'm looking for your father."

CHAPTER 10

A COLD SUNDAY NIGHT in December 1988. A woman answered the phone. "Hi, is Jake Lamar in?" I asked.

"Just a minute please. May I ask who's calling?"

"This is his son Jake."

"Hold on just a second."

My father sounded drunk when he said hello.

"Dad."

"Hey, man, I was gonna call you."

"You were?"

"She told me you called. She wrote your number down and I swear I was gonna call you."

"How is that possible, Dad? You haven't talked to me in five and a half years."

"Naw, man, come on, what are you talking about?"

"Dad, do you know who you're talking to?"

"Isn't this Bert?"

"No, Dad. You have another son. This is Jake. Remember me?"

A long silence. "I remember you," my father said, his voice breaking. "You're the great one. The tremendous one."

"Thank you."

"I cry about you."

"I've thought about you a lot too."

"I read you every week."

"You do?"

"Of course. You're doing great. I'm proud of you."

In that instant, the last twelve years melted away and I was fifteen again. Dad was proud of me. Nothing could have made me happier.

Then he said: "You still have to get that Ph.D. though."

"Uh, Dad," I said, stunned, "I don't think that's going to happen."

"No, no, no. I know you're doing well and all that. I just want you to do *better*."

We made a date to meet at two-thirty the next afternoon at the junior college where he taught. As I hung up the phone, I realized I had not even mentioned the private investigator to Dad. It occurred to me that the call from the detective was just an impetus, a tidy rationale for doing what I had needed to do for a long time. Though I was not going into the *Time* office that Monday, I still put on the clothes I would wear to my job. I wanted to look the way my father would want me to look.

I rode the subway to a part of the Bronx I hadn't visited in years, a busy commercial district, bursting with sound and color, where run-down apartment buildings were sandwiched between an array of discount stores and bodegas. Young black and Hispanic mothers pushed children in strollers. Clusters of old men stood in doorways, drinking out of brown paper bags, arguing in Spanish.

I arrived ten minutes late and found Dad sitting alone in a classroom. He smiled broadly and rose from his desk. We embraced. The flesh on his face seemed looser. His potbelly looked twice as large as before. When he turned his head, I noticed his bald spot had expanded too. But the boisterous laugh, the booming voice, the cold intelligence in the eyes, the powerful aura around him—these were the same. We made small talk as if only a few weeks had passed since we'd last seen each other. There was an almost surreal, dreamy quality about seeing my father again; I felt as if I were in a trance.

Dad showed me around the college. In the computer workroom, we ran into a couple of other teachers. "This is Jake Jr.," Dad said. "He's an associate editor at *Time* magazine. He graduated Harvard *cum laude.* Of course, it should have been *summa cum laude,* but he got lazy." Only my father laughed at his quip. He took me by the faculty room, where we encountered more of his colleagues. "This is Jake Jr. He's an associate editor at *Time* magazine. He graduated Harvard *cum laude.* Of course, it should have been *summa cum laude,* but he got lazy." My father introduced me to two more groups of people and each time he said the exact same thing; and each time he chuckled dryly while his colleagues' smiles turned from surprised to puzzled and I struggled to keep a pleasant expression on my face, though I felt almost as if I were being slapped.

We caught a cab and Dad directed the driver to an address in the Bronx. "I thought you lived in Yonkers," I said.

"I live in a few places," Dad replied. "You know what they used to say in Shingley, Georgia. It's a poor rabbit that don't got but one hole." Dad explained that we were stopping at the home of his girlfriend Marian's mother. Once Marian—who, it turned out, was the niece of an old friend of Dad's—got off from work, the three of us would go to their place in Yonkers for dinner.

"Sorry, Dad," I said. "I have to be back in Manhattan by seven-thirty."

"Oh," my father said. "I thought you were coming over for dinner."

"No, I didn't know that was what you were thinking."

My father turned and looked out the taxi window. "I thought you were staying for dinner," he said, sounding disappointed.

"Sorry, Dad, but I never said that. You never mentioned dinner either."

"Okay."

I asked my father about his teaching. He told me about the courses in business and accounting he led at three different community colleges. His students, he boasted, had the highest GPAs in the schools. "There are so many minorities here," Dad said. "Black and Puerto Rican kids who *want* to learn, they really do. And I have dedicated myself to making them make it. I don't know if I can turn 'em into Harvard—but if anybody can do it, *I* can! I figured I helped mine get through, now I'm going to help all the minorities I can. It's like I'm on a mission."

Dad told me he also managed a dry cleaners in the Bronx and was saving up for his retirement. "I'm not as young as I used to be," he said quietly.

We arrived at our destination. The tenement was crumbling, but the apartment itself was comfortable and familiar, reminding me of the homes of aunts and uncles. There were plastic slipcovers on the couch and chairs; the TV was tuned to a soap opera; I caught the aroma of flour and cooking oil from the kitchen. A plaque on the wall was inscribed with a saying by W.C. Fields: "If at first you don't succeed, try, try again. Then quit. There's no use being a damned fool about it." On the coffee table and bookshelves were neat stacks of *Time* magazine. Marian's mother, Harriet, was a short, wise-eyed woman in pink foam hair curlers. She said she was just about to fry some chicken; would I like some? "Fried chicken is that boy's favorite thing to eat," Dad said before I could answer. "Ain't that right, Jakie?"

"That's right."

We followed Harriet into the kitchen and Dad gave her a strong, affectionate hug from behind. "Harriet here looks after me," my father said. "She keeps me straight. Holds on to my money for me so I don't spend it all. Keeps me from drinking too much. Ain't that right, Harriet?"

"Shut up with your nonsense, Billy," Harriet said matter-of-factly, "and get out a my kitchen."

Dad threw his head back in laughter. "Can you believe this woman talks to me like that? She can be your new grandmother."

"I'm happy with the one I've got, thanks." I didn't so much state this as mutter it under my breath, barely audibly, like an adolescent.

"What do you want on your plate, honey?" Harriet asked me.

"He likes what I like," Dad said grandly. "Fix him everything you fix for me."

My father and I returned to the living room where he poured us full glasses of scotch. We stared into the TV, pretending to be interested in the soap opera as we talked. Or rather, Dad talked. He was thrilled by George Bush's victory in the presidential election a month earlier. "At last we're gonna have a real president." I winced. "I know you don't agree with me," Dad said quickly.

I mentioned the call from the private investigator. My father shrugged it off. "He can find me if he wants. I ain't afraid. I haven't done anything wrong or illegal." Dad told me how his white associates had swindled him out of hundreds of thousands of dollars and consequently wiped out his business. As in the old days, I started to tune out when my father went into the intricacies of his transactions, but I noticed that Dad kept coming back to the same point: he had trusted the wrong people. "The white folks didn't want to see a nigger cutting deals the size I was cutting. A nigger like me, tossing around millions of dollars? Sheeeeet. The white folks didn't like that. I'm just a poor little ole country boy from Georgia, an escapee from the garbage can!" But he bounced back, Dad said, just as he always had. "You know what they say in Shingley, Georgia. Got to keep on keepin' on. And that's what I be doin'. Keep on keepin' on!"

My father launched into the old stories—"Of course, I'm ninety-six years old"—and I realized that in the three hours we'd been together, after not seeing each other for more than half a decade, Dad had not asked me a single question about my life. It was our old pattern, of course, but it surprised me that he could be so incurious after all these years. Did he care where I lived or how I liked my job or how the family had fared without him? When I tried to bring up such things that afternoon, to offer some information, he had abruptly cut me off, changing the subject. More scotch was poured. I had no idea how much we'd drunk at that point but as I got woozier, my father grew louder.

Marian arrived. She was a small-boned, delicate-looking woman with a rich, dark complexion like my grandmother's. She had thought I was coming to Yonkers with them. I told her I never said I was staying for dinner. "Ah," Marian said, a twinkle in her eyes, "he put words in your mouth, did he? I know what that's like."

Marian sat down and Dad poured her a glass of scotch. He told me how he'd won Marian a promotion to head nurse in her department at the Bronx hospital where she worked. "Her boss had retired and instead of appointing Marian *that day* like they should have, they were fuckin' around looking for somebody else. So I just got on the phone and told the director of the hospital what a fucking idiot he was if he didn't promote Marian. And guess what?"

"She got the job."

"She got the job!"

"It was a bit more complicated than that," Marian said with a smile.

"And after I did it," Dad said, pointing at her, "that bitch over there—"

The word was like a glass shattering. Marian just looked at my father and said, "Excuse me?"

"Ooops," Dad chuckled in mock sheepishness like a chastened schoolboy. "Sorry, sweetheart."

"Do you talk to your girlfriends like that?" Marian asked me.

"No, I don't."

"Hey, man," Dad said, "you got to keep these women in line. It's like they used to say in Shingley. You've heard of Shingley, Georgia, haven't you? Population fifteen—"

Marian and I looked at each other and said in unison, "Including the cows and the chickens." We burst into laughter.

Dad broke in. "She thinks my children don't like me! Can you believe that, Jakie? Marian thinks y'all don't *like* me. I told her, I was a father *and* a mother to y'all!"

I stared at the pattern on the rug, unable to speak, while my father talked on. What stories had he told Marian? What stories had he told himself? I felt suddenly as if Dad were sucking all the oxygen out of the room, leaving the rest of us gasping. My father must not only dominate you, he must obliterate you, negate your self, crowd you out of existence. Were other people real to him? Did we have feelings? Perhaps this was the single hardest thing for a human being to do: to look beyond oneself, to imagine what it was like to be in the skin, in the mind, in the heart of another, to fully acknowledge another's humanity. How else could one commit violence against the innocent? Deny the existence of a parent or a child? Or trivialize a person's life in a magazine? Or spit in the face of love? I was trying to see into my father, to break through my own hurt and anger and isolation so that I might pierce his, to see him in his specificity, not as a hero or a monster, but simply as a man, one who would probably remain forever unknowable to me. I wanted to accept him as a man, but I didn't know if I could. And was he capable of accepting me, not as an abstraction—a byline in *Time* magazine, a list of credentials, a child who "liked" him but whom he never saw—but whole and in detail?

"So when are you gonna get your Ph.D.?" my father asked.

"Probably never," I said.

Dad shook his head. "Nope. You've got to get a doctorate."

"What am I gonna get a doctorate in, Dad? They don't give Ph.D.'s in writing."

"Get it in anything," he said, his voice rising. "But you have got to get that piece of paper!"

"Why? What could I possibly need it for?"

"You'll never get to be president without a Ph.D."

"Be serious, Dad. Ronald Reagan is a moron who went to a college nobody ever heard of and he's president. Besides, when did I ever say I wanted to be president? Never. Not once."

"You still have to get that piece of paper!" Dad exploded.

"Why? Just because *you* want me to?" I had to speak rapidly to keep my voice from shaking. "It's not going to happen, Dad. I'm a writer. That's what I do. Now you can either accept that or not but that's the way it is."

"I have a say in this!"

"Actually, Dad," I said as evenly as I could, "you don't."

My father seemed to recoil in his chair. "Look," he said, his voice turning almost plaintive, "if I had stayed in school and gotten my Ph.D. instead of dropping out to support your mother and y'all, there's no telling how far I coulda gone. When I go looking for jobs at universities now, they turn me down because I never got my Ph.D."

"Yeah, well, when I want a job I just tell 'em I went to Harvard and I get it."

My father looked stricken. "Okay, fine," he said shortly. "Let's not discuss it anymore. We're only going to get upset. No point in that." My father folded up now. He didn't want to talk. He didn't want to look at me. He wanted me gone, out of his sight, away.

I felt like shit, stunned by my own cruelty. To use my Harvard education—something Dad had wanted so badly to give me, something he surely could have had himself if only he'd been born in the right time and place—as a weapon against my father, a way of one-upping him, seemed the most mean and shallow thing I could have done. I thought of all the years I had worried about turning into my father—now it seemed I had become something far worse: a self-important buppie, the corporate Tom my father had refused to be, proudly proclaiming myself a writer when all I did was hack for a newsmagazine. Who was I to judge my father so harshly? Dad went into the inner city every day and tried to help our people, to educate them, to give them the tools to succeed. Did I do anything even remotely as significant as that? All the years I had damned my father for his blindness to himself and to others—what about me? What depths of denial and self-justification did I swim in just to make it through a day, to live with my contradictions? I had come to see my father in search of some resolution, but the mystery of both of us had only deepened. Was it possible that we could love each other, admire each other, and still be unable to bear sitting in the same room together?

After a long, uncomfortable silence, Marian showed me a picture of her grandchild. She told me how playful Dad was with the baby, how the little boy lit up whenever my father was around. "I've got another little rabbit," Dad said softly. That was what he had called my sister when she was a child, his little rabbit. And I realized that Dad, just as he had with Ruth, her mother and children, had found himself another surrogate family. I wondered if this was the family that would be with him when he died.

It was seven o'clock. Marian offered to drive me back to Manhattan. As we put on our coats to leave, my father bragged about me to Harriet. "He was president of the student body," Dad said. "I wrote his speech for him. He was always the best. That's what I demanded." Then, grinning inscrutably, my father said, "And I only had to beat him once."

Driving into Manhattan, I sat beside Marian in the passenger seat, but my father controlled the conversation from the back of the car. I barely listened. Marian dropped me off at the corner of 72nd and Columbus. "I do hope you'll come to our place for dinner sometime soon," she said.

"I'd like that," I said.

My father stepped out of the car to switch to the passenger seat. We stood on the corner, face to face. "All right, man," he said, "take it easy."

We shook hands. "Bye, Daddy."

Watching the taillights of Marian's car fade down 72nd Street, I felt utterly lonely, and untethered at last.

"So it wasn't *The Cosby Show*," Roy said with a compassionate sigh. "What did you expect?"

"I don't know," I said, sitting on the other end of my couch, two nights after I had seen my father. "Something . . . else."

We were quiet for a while. "So—are you gonna call him again?" Roy asked.

"I don't know. Maybe. Eventually. Not anytime soon."

"Will he call you?"

"Never."

"You're sure about that?"

"Yes."

I paused. Roy, watching me, said, in a voice I knew he probably used with his clients, "Continue."

"I think I understand one thing about my father."

"What?"

"He did the best he could."

"Which is all he could have done."

"And, if I had grown up under his circumstances, I doubt I could have done any better . . . And, given my own circumstances, I might someday do a hell of a lot worse."

"You won't."

"I've decided, though, that I'm gonna have to quit my job soon."

Roy looked surprised. "And do what?"

"Write what I want to write."

"Or need to write."

Roy left to catch the subway back to his apartment in Brooklyn around midnight. I was too wired to sleep. I felt as if a door had flung open on a dark room. I wanted to find out what was inside, hoping that I might discover definition; wondering if perhaps the searching in the dark itself was what might define me; not knowing if I had the skill or the nerve to try to make the search mean anything to anybody, but knowing that, at the very least, if fate or God or dumb luck allowed, I'd always have Roy to talk to about it.

One o'clock and I still wasn't tired. I pulled a pen and a fresh notebook from the file cabinet and, employing one of my father's better methods for dealing with insomnia, sat down at the table and got to work.